The Inner Child in Dreams

A C. G. JUNG FOUNDATION BOOK

Published in association with Daimon Verlag
Einsiedeln, Switzerland

The C. G. Jung Foundation for Analytical Psychology is dedicated to helping men and women to grow in conscious awareness of the psychological realities in themselves and society, find healing and meaning in their lives and greater depth in their relationships, and to live in response to their discovered sense of purpose. It welcomes the public to attend its lectures, seminars, films, symposia, and workshops and offers a wide selection of books for sale through its bookstore. The Foundation also publishes *Quadrant*, a semiannual journal, and books on Analytical Psychology and related subjects. For information about Foundation programs or membership, please write to the C.G. Jung Foundation, 28 East 39th Street, New York, NY 10016.

THE
INNER CHILD
IN DREAMS

KATHRIN ASPER

Translated by Sharon E. Rooks

SHAMBHALA
Boston & London
1992

Shambhala Publications, Inc.
Horticultural Hall
300 Massachusetts Avenue
Boston, Massachusetts 02115
www.shambhala.com

Printed in the United States of America

Distributed in the United States by Random House, Inc., and in Canada by Random House of Canada Ltd

LIBRARY OF CONGRESS CATALOGING-IN-PUBLICATION DATA

Asper, Kathrin, 1941–
    [Von der Kindheit zum Kind in uns. English]
    The inner child in dreams/Kathrin Asper.—1st ed.
        p.   cm.
    Translation of: Von der Kindheit zum Kind in uns.
    "A C. G. Jung Foundation/Daimon book."
    Includes bibliographical references.
    ISBN 1-57062-679-0 (pbk.: acid-free)
    1. Children in dreams.   2. Inner child.   I. Title.
    BF1099.C53A87   1991   90-50823
    154.6'32—dc20   CIP
BVG 01

Contents

Preface

THIS BOOK deals with the motif of the child in our dreams. In approaching this topic, I began by asking what meanings could be assigned to the various images of children that arise in dreams. To familiarize myself with the material, I collected and examined many dreams, and, in the course of time, the major spheres of meaning crystalized. The symbol of the child points to something new and future-oriented; it can have a religious meaning; and finally it can symbolize creative possibilities.

Working with these dreams also led in the end to the question of how our own childhood is dealt with in dreams. From this arose the interesting observation that dreams are seldom directly concerned with us as the child we once were. On the contrary, they make use of various kinds of devices to veil the events of childhood. For this reason, special therapeutic and psychological considerations are required to enable us to learn about our childhood through dreams.

The dreams presented here as a rule deal not with our literal offspring but rather with our own inner child, with the child that we once were, with our spontaneous, childlike aspects and our future possibilities. The child is an extremely important symbol in dreams, one that not only mirrors our nature and our temperament, but also often provides hints about how we can structure our lives more productively.

Learning to understand our own inner child and taking up the dialogue with the child that we once were are essential steps in getting to know ourselves better. Understanding "how it all came about" also enables us to embrace the future more innocently, more spontaneously, and more freely, living more fully in the process.

Here I want to thank all those who permitted me to use their dreams and to include crucial details about their lives. I feel richly rewarded by these contributions. Personal details have been changed to ensure anonymity.

My thanks also go to Dr. Mario Jacoby, who took the trouble to read and comment on the manuscript.

KATHRIN ASPER
Meilen
August 1987

Introduction

FEW SYMBOLS bring together opposites the way that of the child does. On the one hand, the child is the most holy image that exists; for example, there is the Christ Child. On the other hand, the divine child is also exposed to grisly dangers like the Massacre of the Innocents in Bethlehem. It is noteworthy, however, that the latter theme does not appear very often in the visual arts. Leafing through art books, even those concerned exclusively with depictions of children, or going through museums and art galleries with a particular eye to representations of Madonna and Child, one is struck by one key point: there are few if any pictures in which the Child is shown screaming and crying, making a fuss, being disobedient. Everywhere it is the idyllic bond between mother and child and the blessed innocence of the child that the artist has captured. And yet who knows better than parents that children are not just angels, but also—and sometimes mainly—unbearably obstinate, spiteful, and aggressive.

Folk literature is far more familiar than the visual arts with defiant, lazy, burdensome, and hard-hearted children. We might recall the cold, self-serving, evil "Pitch Mary" in the Grimm's tale "Mother Holle." The title character in "Lazy Heinz" is another example: he is so lazy that he can barely manage to take care of his only goat. In "Mother Trude" a cheeky and obstinate young girl asks so many nerve-wracking questions that Mother Trude turns her into a piece of firewood and burns her. Obstinacy is punished in fairy tales: the baby in "The Raven" is cursed by her royal mother because she cannot keep still, and later turns into a raven.

Still, we find on closer examination that even in fairy tales nasty children are not a frequent occurrence. Even here there seems to be a need to put the emphasis on the good child. The extent to which this tendency corresponds with a human predisposition becomes quite clear in the Grimm's tale "Eve's Unequal Children," in which the first parents are awaiting a visit from God. Eve dresses up her beautiful children and hides the ugly ones. Not until God is generously blessing the nice children does Eve remember the other ones, fetch "the whole crude, dirty, scabby, grimy band" out of hiding, and present them to the Lord. Benevolently, He also blesses these children. In other words, God Himself has to make an effort before we take pleasure in ill-bred children; they have no unconditional guarantee of human affection.

Today, adults are more tolerant of disobedient little children, in whom we recognize the first valuable beginnings of autonomy and independence. If we take to heart the teachings of psychology over the last decade, we know that suppressing or overcontrolling a child's individual efforts can lead to serious developmental disturbances, and thus we handle our children's stubbornness more carefully than our parents did.

In the visual arts, as I have observed, there are very few portrayals of crying, disobedient, cross children, compared with those of innocent, charming youngsters. Two pictures by famous artists come spontaneously to mind. One is a chalk drawing by the Renaissance artist Albrecht Dürer showing an irritable, crying cherub.[1] During the Renaissance, the stylized depiction and gold ground of medieval art receded, and the individual, realistic portrait became important. The human being in his or her concrete individuality and enmeshment in society became the focus of interest.

It is thus no accident that precisely during this period artists began to capture the unpleasant expressions of children and so shattered the myth of the holy, innocent child. The Dutch painters of the seventeenth and eighteenth centuries were even more drawn to the spontaneous, naughty, and sometimes hard-to-tolerate aspect of the child's nature. A pen-and-ink sketch by Rembrandt, *The Naughty Child* (fig. 1), is a good example. The wriggling, flailing child is placed unequivocally in the cen-

FIGURE 1
The Naughty Child by Rembrandt. Kupferstichkabinett Staatliche Museen,
Preussischer Kulturbesitz, Berlin.

ter. It is obvious that it is so ill-behaved that the mother has no choice but to get him out of the room. Rembrandt captured this state of affairs with a few quick pen strokes, thus portraying for us a familiar, recurring event.

However, true-to-life depictions of this kind should not be permitted to hide the fact that the myth of the innocent, beautiful, loving child remained intact into modern times and continues up to the present day. Artists persist in attributing the qualities of ideal beings to children, as being closer to the source of life than adults. In connection with this I am reminded of a song—which may stand for so many similar ones—with the title "Just for One Day," by Peter Maffay, a popular German singer well known in Europe:

> Once more I would like to be a child
> Just for one day
> Once more not to have to defend myself
> Just for one day
> Once more not to have to decide anything
> Just for one day
> Once more to be able to love everything
> Just for one day
> Once more I would like to be a child
> Just for one day
> Once more not to have to hide anything
> Just for one day
> Once more not to need to lie
> Just for one day
> Once more to be able to say everything
> Just for one day

> Refrain:
> As I go to sleep at night
> I laugh in my dream
> Because I put all my trust
> In the new day
> Feel myself rested and wide-awake
> In the first light of dawn.[2]

The lyrics describe childhood as paradise and endow the child with qualities that stand in stark contrast to the behavior of adults. The child is rarely forced to defend himself, needs to decide nothing, loves everything, does not have to hide and lie. He laughs in his dreams, trusts the new day, and is full of vitality. The song not only describes an ideal child, but expresses a way of being upon which are projected all the wishes of the heavy-laden adult who yearns for childhood. Maffay speaks to the hidden longing of many people who have grown weary of hopelessness, mistrust, war, restlessness, and exhaustion.

From time immemorial, throughout the world, the child has been the bearer of our deepest longings and highest ideals. Holiness, innocence, harmony, happiness, pleasure and joy, peace and eternity, are all equally projected onto the child, and he appears in art, literature, mythology, and religion as a being blessed with all the characteristics of divinity. The child as symbol mirrors not outer reality but rather the inner reality of the psyche and reflects the wishes, hopes, and longings to which we aspire. Thus the child becomes a symbol for that which is new and yet to come.

This spiritual level of meaning stands in sharp contrast to the actuality of the child's existence. If one believes the sensational accounts of the past ten years by writers such as Philippe Ariès, the history of childhood is one long horror story in which abuse, abandonment, intentional starvation, murder, neglect, atrocious swaddling practices, and educational methods harmful to both body and soul were legion. Only rarely are other ways of dealing with children found in history. I am reminded, for example, of artistic representations of children by the Greeks, who succeeded quite early in capturing the nature and characteristics of children in their sculpture, painting (especially on vases and pitchers), and grave stelae.[3] An appealing and striking instance of their unusual attitude toward children is the grave stele of the small Plangon from the Munich Glyptothek (fig. 2). The little girl stands with her back against the right edge, holding "a small bird in her lowered left hand and a doll in her raised right hand. She faces a goose on the left, which trustingly extends its head and foot toward her. On the wall hangs a large bone pouch [children used to play with bones] and beside it, a doll's dress.

FIGURE 2

Grave stele (325/20 B.C.). Munich Glyptothek.

The picture tells us in detail what was dear to this child in life and which games brought her happiness."[4]

We should not let the increasing empathy, in our time, for the child's psyche and needs blind us to the fact that even today children are victims of the most cruel practices. Child abuse cases are unfortunately increasing at an alarming rate and are sometimes fatal or so serious that the child requires hospitalization. It has been estimated that between 30,000 and 80,000 cases of child abuse occurred in West Germany in 1982.[5] However, these numbers appear to make up only the tip of the iceberg, since the number of unreported cases must be assumed to be far higher. Also alarming is the fact that telephone hotlines for children have had to be set up in various locations and have been used by them for serious emergencies.

The abandoned and endangered child is a theme of the hero myths of every era. In these, however, the children survive thanks to the help of the elements. Water, for example, carries them away from danger and toward a merciful fate and a happy existence. This was the case with Moses, who was entrusted to the river in his basket, and of the hero of the Grimm's fairy tale "The Devil with the Three Golden Hairs." The abandoned child of myth overcomes danger because Mother Nature intervenes and protects him with her powers; in addition to his own mother, the heroic child always knows the transpersonal mother, nature, which saves him from ruin.

Even in the real world children can withstand a difficult beginning in life and not necessarily be destroyed by it. But there are many who continue to suffer from the profound injuries resulting from an unfavorable beginning in life and lack of mothering. This can weigh heavily on their lives for a long time, and their existence seems to repeat the misfortune of their beginning in successive difficulties. They live out the motif of the abandoned child in all its shadings and variations. We need only ask social workers about the lives of the children in their care, or read the medical histories of people in psychiatric clinics, or look into the life stories of criminals to see that childhood can be terrible. The circumstances are not necessarily always drastic and concrete; sometimes the situation is more subtle. The so-called "happy childhood" and "good background" on closer examination frequently reveal extensive abandonment and neglect.[6]

It often takes a long time for an individual to realize what happened in his or her childhood. Freud called attention to this by saying that the events and experiences of childhood have to be extricated from repression. Things that we experienced as unpleasant when we were children are pushed away. The process of repression is reinforced by the rapid passage of years and the future-related orientation of young people. Parents make an important contribution toward repression in that the child often believes what they say more than his or her own experience. Goethe effectively formulated this idea in his autobiography when he wrote, "When a person tries to remember what happened in the earliest time of his youth, it often happens that he confuses what he has heard from others with what he actually possesses from his own conscious experience."[7]

The child we once were must be rediscovered so that we can find the point of connection with our actual experience. Not only is this a therapeutic axiom of many psychological movements and schools, but also, I believe, it is in the nature of being human, an inherent need to take stock of one's life at one time or another, to look back and inquire into one's origins. The many memoirs of childhood and youth that have been published—not only in the past, but especially today—bear witness to this need. Writing down early experiences provides a kind of self-therapy. As the poet Heinrich Heine wrote: "Sickness was no doubt the ultimate reason / For the whole creative impulse; / In creating I could be healed; / In creating I became healthy."

The primary importance of examining one's childhood is that in this way a connection to the essential pattern of one's life can be found. Many people experience themselves as alienated from themselves[8] and find that the "path marked out for them by nature" is not so simple as Goethe assumed when he wrote: "No matter which way a person may turn, no matter what enterprises he might embark on, he will always return to the path that nature first marked out for him."[9]

Many people need therapy in order to pursue this humanistic ideal of self-development. In the psychological process of finding the child in oneself again and becoming aware of the wholeness of one's nature that this child represents, one makes use of dreams. Sometimes dreams can provide important information about the inner child and his or her experiences.

However, since our childhood often lies sheltered far from consciousness, specific difficulties arise in working with the symbol of the child in dreams. Only very rarely do dreams tell about the child we once were in a direct and undisguised way. A dream such as the following, which brings up a key childhood event in a completely unmasked manner, is a rarity. A middle-aged women dreamed:

> I am sitting as a small child in a baby stroller, and my father is pushing the stroller. He is wearing a long black coat. The handle of the stroller slips out of his grasp, and the stroller keeps going on its own. I am terribly frightened. My father shouts angrily, "Stop, stop!"

For the dreamer this dream memory had a guiding and illuminating effect. It confirmed a suspicion that had already been discussed in many sessions of analysis. The dream portrayed an event that, as she now seemed to remember, actually took place, and it confirmed the assumption that her father had expected too much of her when she was a small child and also probably had blamed her for his own failures and mistakes. His shout to the child to stop the stroller is absurd—how could a little child stop her own stroller?—but it also transfers the blame to the child.

Both the child that once was and childhood itself appear in a veiled form in dreams: they may be shifted onto other dream figures, sometimes appearing not at all or only in a stylized transformation. In chapter 1, "Child and Childhood," I shall discuss this in detail. Chapter 2 deals with the symbol of the child as a symbol of life. In this context I shall also discuss depression, because there exists in the depressive condition, as well as in its end phase, a certain connection to the child symbol in dreams. Chapter 3 deals with the theme of the holy and divine child. There I try to present this difficult topic as realistically as possible. Depression, that enigmatic emotional illness, will be discussed in chapter 3 in its spiritual orientation. In chapter 4 I examine the experience of being a child of God in connection with the themes of the lost faith of childhood and of the filial relationship with God. Chapter 5, about the child in its smiling, playful, and creative aspect, concludes the book. My exposition thus covers the entire spectrum of the child symbol from its relationship with the past to its future-oriented aspect. Yesterday and today, past and future, should be addressed in equal measure in considering the appearance of the child in dreams.

WORKING WITH DREAMS

Dreams are essential for the preservation of our physical and psychological equilibrium. Some people remember their dreams; others do not remember them very well if at all, but the fact is that each of us dreams every night, as dream research has proven.

Remembered sequences of dream images can often give us information about our life and our entanglement with it, because they speak about the past, the present, or the future. By working with our dreams, we become better acquainted with our own inner condition and gain a further reference point beyond those provided by consciousness and the ego functions. Also, dreams are often simply beautiful and impressive. Yet they can be serious, too, as are nightmares from which we may awaken trembling, bathed in perspiration and with a pounding heart.

The images that occur in dreams are often symbols, which must be interpreted symbolically in a way that goes beyond our concrete understanding of them and suggests a deeper meaning that is not so easy to understand. Thus, for example, the child, which appears in many dreams, represents not just a concrete, personified child but is rather a symbol heralding something new and yet to come and suggesting something vital. As a rule the symbolic child has to do with the dreamer himself and symbolizes aspects of his own personality; it is, in other words, an inner child. We call such an interpretation subjective because it has to do with the person who is dreaming, the subject. An interpretation that views the child as a concrete external object is called objective. Subjective and objective interpretations can be extended to all the figures and situations that occur in dreams. In many instances both interpretive approaches can be applied at the same time, each revealing its own meaning.

In considering the various manifestations and meanings of the child in dreams, I also include dreams in which the child does not appear overtly but in which the dreamer experiences himself or herself as a child, daughter or son, and behaves and is treated accordingly.

It is not at all easy to deal with the child motif in dreams, even when one isolates this symbol to some extent from the wealth of other imagery in the dream. All of us who pay attention to our dreams can attest, however, that dreams speak in a thousand tongues and often use different images to indicate the same thing. Thus the dream can express the concept of something new through the child symbol but can also indicate this through the symbol of a plant, with its green color, or through the image of young animals; finally the image of building a house can also indicate impending events. Each of these symbols evokes a different aspect of the theme of newness. If we were to take the child motif alone and isolate it, we would remove it from the richness of meaning that lies in its interconnectedness with the other symbols. This is the danger of isolating a symbol, of overdefining it. If we isolate it, we might easily end up overloading it with too many shades of meaning and overvaluing it in relation to the other symbols that appear in the same context with it in a dream series.

But what is it that justifies the study of a symbol? This discussion of the child in dreams was written with the intention of providing guidelines for people who want to devote more attention to their dreams. The child is such a richly faceted symbol that through it the meaningfulness of dreams can easily be shown. It is, so to speak, a long-term symbol, that is, its effect extends over a long period of time and its meaning can be worked out, even roughly, only through careful observation of the inner and outer situation. This makes longer periods of analysis necessary, which at the same time allows us to take a good look at the psychological processes involved.

We should always bear in mind that the interpretation of a dream is derived not only from the actual dream itself. To produce an interpretation, the analyst makes use of other sources of information: for example, an understanding of the childhood and/or current situation of the dreamer, a knowledge of biographical facts, a perception of the mood of the analysand, his or her gestures and facial experiences, and his or her supplementary remarks about the dream, what strikes him or her about it, plus his knowledge about earlier dreams. Readers who are not in analysis and have no one to discuss their dreams with might best carry their dreams around with them, examine them in their minds, let them drift through their thoughts, and meditate on them, recalling similar events and being open to whatever thoughts arise in thinking about them.

A specific attitude is necessary to understand dreams. I would describe it in the following way: it circles rather than going in a straight line, waits rather than heading directly toward a goal; it consists more in *being* with the dream than in *having* the content of the dream; it accompanies the contents of a dream. People who think in a focused and logical way will experience this attitude as vague, and indeed it is. Here one must have the courage to endure the vagueness until a certainty about the message of the dream is arrived at by means of patiently keeping company with the dreams and one's hunches about them until one's consciousness changes imperceptibly through their influence and—suddenly, or so it seems to consciousness, though consistently for the process—new insights come to light, something new is grasped, the old is elucidated, and what is happening now becomes more understandable.

The approach to dreams that I have described is one that does not fit in at all with our traditional patriarchal thinking. It is not father-oriented; that is, it does not go forward step by step with the goal of arriving at a clear answer. I would much rather call this approach mother-oriented.

On the other hand, the vagueness of the dream message should not lead to the false assumption that there is nothing definite in dreams. Something definite might well be there too. This reminds me of the account given by a simple farmer's wife who had dreamed that a child was about to be born. She took the dream seriously, stayed up later than usual the next evening, and, guided by the dream, prepared hot water and towels. At a late hour there was a knock at the door and a young couple stood outside. The woman was well advanced in pregnancy and had started to go into labor. The couple had been unable to get back to the valley in time from their vacation house and had knocked at her house, where they saw a light. The farmer's wife was ready and helped the pregnant woman deliver a healthy child.

This example shows the importance of inspiration. This woman acted on her inspiration and was very close to the knowledge of dreams. Seldom does a person of our times who is oriented toward patriarchal values have this degree of closeness to the unconscious. For this reason it is better for most of us not to give immediate credence to our quick dream interpretations, because we are operating from superimposed patterns of thought of the "father-oriented" type. As a result we might come up with a number of dream interpretations without there being a single one that speaks to us on the feeling level. In my opinion the most fruitful approach is to let all of these interpretations remain side by side so that we can then quite gradually connect with the hidden knowledge of the dream message in a "mother-oriented" way. Then, when we "know," our knowledge is not a product of rational patterns of thought but is instead felt as a certainty. Dream interpretation is effective when it reaches our feelings. All other dream interpretations are comparable to the endless variety of combinations in a kaleidoscope. They are merely the play of confusion and remain so until certainty on the feeling level has arisen as to what is of real concern to the individual in question. The certainty of feeling and trust in our feelings are crucial aids in understanding a dream and its message.

1 The Child and Childhood in Dreams

MANY PEOPLE feel they have been cheated out of their childhood. Although it cannot be claimed that we are entitled to a happy childhood, we do have the right to complain about an unhappy one, to mourn it, and then to take on the difficult task of integrating our childhood, of taking our parents off the pedestal of omnipotence and godliness and seeing them as people like ourselves. Such steps can free us to affirm our inner child and allow us to live life spontaneously.

In this chapter I shall first describe the aspects of an analysis in relation to the child and childhood motifs as they appear in dreams. This approach provides the possibility of reflecting the richness of what happens in analysis and offers a condensed but largely complete account of the complex process involved. Both general and individual points of view about the theme of integrating one's childhood are discussed here in connection with dreams that provided guidance and were often prefigurations of future events. There are two additional sections, one dealing with the influence on the child of his fantasies about his parents and the other with the theme of the sick child.

A CHILD WHO WAS NOT PERMITTED TO BE A CHILD

When I look back on Bernhard and his analysis, I find that above all the image of a person who felt cheated out of his childhood has carved itself into my memory.

Bernhard was twenty-four years old when he came to see me. He wanted to get to know himself better and in the first session described his problems with his parents. He also talked about his feeling of always doing everything wrong. His manner of speaking was hesitant; with each long pause he once more sunk resignedly into a tense silence.

As it turned out, Bernhard suffered from a strong negative father complex. He had an excessive attachment to his father, and because of this he experienced the paternal quality as extremely negative wherever he encountered it—in his own mother, in authority figures, or in institutions. A father complex (and this is true in general for all complexes) is always multilayered and can never be traced back to the personal father alone or to any single source of influence. For Bernhard the father complex meant, first of all, that he was excessively controlled by fatherly qualities, which he experienced as negative and life-denying. Linked to this was the fact that he distrusted irrationality and emotional experiences, and had inadequate access to his own feminine capacity for feeling. He appeared to have experienced too little of the positive feminine-maternal element in his childhood, because his mother had completely subordinated herself to his father and was herself committed to strong objective values. Bernhard had the appearance of an emotionally paralyzed and imprisoned man. This was reflected in his symptoms of fear and claustrophobia, asthma attacks, and dejected, depressive moods. Subjectively he viewed himself as a failure; he was inhibited and unsure of himself, and felt himself to be the object of continuous critical observation and judgment.

The atmosphere of Bernhard's childhood home was dominated by established middle-class values, which laid great stress on external conformity to society's standards. This orientation toward collective values took on even more weight at the time the family moved to Switzerland, when Bernhard and his siblings were still young. As foreigners they had to pay particular attention to the customs and traditions of their new country. Both parents embraced a self-righteous Protestantism; indeed, according to Bernhard, the religiosity of his mother bordered on fanaticism. The children were constantly encouraged to be model children. The parents treated them as objects to show off in front of relatives and friends. Bernhard and his brothers and sisters adapted effortlessly to their parents' demands: for example, they set the breakfast table every Sunday morning of their own accord. In addition, Bernhard was only allowed to go out in the evenings after he turned twenty. It was Bernhard's feeling that they always had to be thankful; by means of gratitude and obedience the children ensured their parents' love.

The ideals fostered in the home were perfection, a sense of duty, purity, courage, tradition, and, above all, absolute obedience to parents and God. Feelings were given little attention and had to be repressed. Bernhard remembered being left alone often. His parents made fun of him for being afraid of the dark. Once, when the family went for a walk at dusk, his parents hid behind a woodpile and intentionally frightened him to rid him of his silly fear. He also remembered their simply throwing away his pacifier one day without even noticing his tears. An incident with a dearly beloved teddy bear affected him even more deeply. When he was about six years old, his mother threw the bear into the furnace one day, supposedly because it had gotten dirty and unsightly. In his view his mother had cruelly robbed him of a consoling companion.

Bernhard was also terrified of a particular brook as a child. His father, wanting to break him of this unmanly fear, held him over the water. The boy panicked and screamed wildly without getting any sympathy from his parents. The child's need for freedom received little consideration. Drastic punishment resulted when he did not come directly home from school or when he rode his bicycle outside the area designated by his parents. The bicycle was then taken away from him for four weeks. Bernhard remembered that, through a telephone network, his parents always knew where the children were, and it never took long to set the telephone contacts in motion. When the children went sledding in a nearby meadow in the winter, the father watched from the balcony with his binoculars and was able to enumerate all their spills and pranks when they got home. Bernhard was not allowed to bring friends home with him. He often felt lonely for this reason, and eventually he made up games for two children and played them with an imaginary companion.

Regarding his current situation, I learned that he had recently moved out of his parents' house against their wishes and now, equally to his parents' displeasure, was living with his girl-friend. Although he had recently completed his training as a telephone engineer, he didn't want to work for an institution. He felt strongly threatened by bureaucracy and company politics, revolted against them, and finally found it preferable to take odd jobs far below the level of his training. He wanted to be free and unrestrained and began to live the life of a dropout, espousing values contrasting with traditional ones. The values he lived by as a dropout, however, were quite strongly influenced by para-dise fantasies typical of unrealistic ideologies. Thus his rela-tionship to the present was characterized by rage and an attitude of revolt but also by uncertainty, anxiety, and retreat, and by excessive paradisaic imaginations and a longing for a world restored to unity. It seemed to me that in his revolt, Bernhard was making up for delayed adolescent rebellion. In addition I had the impression that his uncertainty and fear must have shaped his experience of childhood. Rage and helplessness were probably a part of his experience as a child, but appropriate expression of these feelings had most certainly never been al-lowed; they had to be repressed. Bernhard experienced his cur-rent environment as an expression of restrictive parental figures; thus his own sad version of his childhood was reproduced again and again. The child he had been lived on inside him, full of rage, anxiety, and helplessness, but also in his yearnings for a better world. This child who had never been listened to deter-mined the course of Bernhard's life, leading him into situations that resembled those of his childhood. Only in this way could the child, of which Bernhard himself was still unconscious, tell his story and let it be known that he felt he had been excessively tyrannized and cheated out of his childhood.

At the beginning of analysis Bernhard firmly rejected the idea just expressed that the former child within him was crying out for acknowledgment and recognition. He was to a great extent unconscious of these connections. He did not know that when he railed against the military and other authorities, he was basi-cally rebelling against the father figures of his childhood, embodied in his own father and in the patriarchal value system of his mother. Yesterday and today were not separated in his experience, and so his analysis would entail bringing about a separation of past from present, allowing him a right to his own life, at which point he could begin to live more spontaneously.

The first dream that Bernhard brought to analysis was this one:

> Children are sledding. I notice angrily that one of them turns over; I find it completely unnecessary. Then I come with other people to a hill where many people are gathered near a tree. Someone asks me why I am not in the military. Then suddenly a man appears who calls a school friend of mine out from the crowd. Apparently he has done something wrong. He is placed face down on a board. Then the man begins to press glowing coals behind my friend's ears with his feet. I do nothing about it.

This dream involves children and a young boy but makes no direct statement about Bernhard's childhood. Yet Bernhard is angered by the inattentiveness of small children, the same response that his father had previously exhibited toward him. The dream shows that his father was also alive in him, that Bernhard had appropriated his father's strictness and identified with it. In the second part of the dream a boy is sadistically punished with hot coals. I was reminded of the time Bernhard's parents frightened him in an equally sadistic way to rid him of his fear of darkness.

This dream refers only indirectly to Bernhard's childhood. None of the many dreams from the beginning phase of his analysis directly involved his experience as a child. However, this phenomenon was not peculiar to Bernhard but is encountered time and again in therapeutic practice: as a rule, dreams do not refer directly to the dreamer as a child nor to his or her childhood experiences. What takes place in dreams confirms Freud's observation that our significant memories are repressed. According to Freud, a "censor" is at work in dreams, displacing and masking affective events so that they can no longer be recognized by consciousness. The same thing happens in connection with our daily life. We remember our own childhood in a biased way, frequently preserving only that which is unimportant, whereas, as Freud put it, "in the adult's memory (frequently, but not always) no trace remains of the important, vivid, and emotion-laden impressions of this period."[1] Childhood memories are often "cover memories" for other really important impressions, which are only revealed through psychological analysis.

This was true in Bernhard's case. Direct memories of his childhood exhausted themselves after a few vivid descriptions, and the child and his experiences appeared in dreams only in an indirect and altered fashion. His father and mother did not appear directly in his dreams for a long time. Fatherly qualities appeared, however, in the form of policemen, school janitors, teachers, ministers, and military men. All had something tyrannical about them that degraded whoever they were dealing with to the level of a child. The following dream shows the pattern:

> At the front of a classroom—it is about the same size as a movie theater—stands a tyrant. Everyone who is sitting in the room knows that moving around in his chair or speaking is forbidden.

Unconsciously the adult Bernhard was still a schoolboy and experienced himself, as he did as a child, as being at the mercy of a destructive superior power. Another of his dreams had to do with the value system that is imposed on a young boy. Bernhard actually experienced this in his own case. Many times as a boy he had wanted to communicate his feelings about his experiences but the people close to him did not validate his feelings and immediately shifted his communication onto an objective, generalized level. This is what happens, for example, when we respond to someone's personal suffering by mouthing some platitude such as "Every cloud has a silver lining." To do this is to abandon the person emotionally, without acknowledging his pain. Patriarchal attitudes are offered too quickly, at the expense of maternal, human concern. Bernhard's upbringing had followed this pattern, leaving him with a feeling of emotional abandonment.

His dream about the imposed value system went as follows:

> I want to be admitted into a foreign country, but someone
> refuses me entry; even at home I am not feeling very well. I
> am constantly being watched by a policeman who threatens
> me with punishments. Then someone else is there, a boy.
> However, it is not only his parents who are scolding the boy;
> his grandmother is also forcing some kind of moral lesson on
> him.

In the dream Bernhard experiences himself as being watched by
the police. This childhood experience is portrayed *as something
going on now*. That is the usual case. We do not dream differently about childhood; on the contrary, in our dreams, things
still are as they were then. Such dreams show how the past
unconsciously intrudes into the present and continues for long
periods to determine our experience of it.

In addition to displacing childhood experiences onto other
people and places, dreams often show the events of childhood in
a general form, *over-elevated onto the archetypal plane*. That
means that important issues are dealt with not in connection
with the people in our everyday lives, but rather in connection
with typical figures from history and mythology. In Bernhard's
case his main complex, a father complex, appeared in the form
of Adolf Hitler, who, in his destructive power, was a symbolic
father figure for an entire era and an entire people:

> With someone else, I am looking at the sky in the dream.
> Suddenly a cloud becomes a face with sharp features. The
> face seems familiar to me, and I recognize first the leader of
> our group but then shortly afterward the face of Adolf Hitler.
> I fear another war could break out.

Adolf Hitler did not play a role in Bernhard's life, as neither
he nor his parents were directly touched by Hitler or the Second
World War. In Bernhard's dream, Hitler represents a collective
factor of destructive power. He appears in the sky, like an
ancient sky god, and so takes on even greater importance. In
another dream it is a thunderstorm, the domain of ancient
weather gods—one thinks of Zeus hurling his lightning bolts—
which threatens Bernhard:

> I am alone in a cabin. A terrible thunderstorm suddenly
> moves overhead. I am terribly afraid. I pray to God to spare
> me. God hears me—or was I just lucky?

In another dream an impersonal iron fist presses down on
Bernhard, preventing him from going on with his life; it is the
iron grip of a huge, unknown force. Here, too, the theme is
raised beyond the everyday level and modified into something
impersonal, so that the destructive element can appear in an
even weightier form:

> I am lying in bed in A——. I would like to get up, but I feel
> an iron fist holding me back. I try again and again, and every
> time the pressure holding me back gets stronger. Finally I
> succeed in fighting my way out of bed. Near the closet the
> grip tightens again, just as when one wants to turn back
> toward shore when the tide is going out. I finally manage to
> escape from the hand. In the hallway I meet my parents and
> want to tell them about my fright. But Father isn't listening at
> all and Mother only with one ear. But there is also a small
> girl, whom I don't know, who is crying: for the first time she
> has heard her own tale of woe.

Bernhard is clearly the underdog in this dream; he is also a
son and not yet an adult. The unconscious here is signifying in
drastic fashion which overpowering forces he feels most threatened by. (I shall say more presently about the girl in this dream.)

Let us pause in our reflections on Bernhard's dreams and pose
three questions of general interest regarding the integration of
childhood.

1. Why is it that in dreams the experience of childhood and
our enmeshment with our parents is not represented directly,
but rather shifted onto other people and often elevated onto an
archetypal level?

As a general rule, the further something is removed from
consciousness, the more in dreams it is shifted onto other figures
and places and appears in unfamiliar form. This is the way our
consciousness protects itself from painful and embarrassing
memories, finding through these displacement mechanisms the
strategies necessary for survival. If we put ourselves in the place

of the child we once were, it becomes perfectly understandable that we repressed our rage, because if we had expressed this feeling, we would have met with our parents' disapproval and rejection. The repression that begins in childhood is therefore unavoidable if one is to live up to the ideology of one's family.

Overelevation of persons, places, and problems onto the archetypal level deserves special attention. Archetypal overelevation also involves displacement and masking: things are transformed into impersonal and typical factors or figures. When, as in Bernhard's case, the personal father does not appear as himself but rather as a thunderstorm, Adolf Hitler, or an iron fist, it means, in the view of Jung's analytical psychology, that the personal parents represent only one side of the truth; the other side is bound up with the father and mother images that are imprinted on the individual psyche and have their effect there independently of the influences of the world around us. These inner images influence our experience of "father" and "mother" as much as our actual parents do. Expressed more simply, this means that a child's experience of the father, for example, is dependent on (a) the inner father image possessed by the individual from birth and (b) the personal father and the fatherly qualities of the people to whom the child relates most closely. Thus a father complex always has, aside from its personal significance, a general, archetypal root and meaning. This perspective provides a breadth of view that goes beyond the merely personal explanation of our childhood. This makes it possible for an individual not to remain stuck in accusations against his parents, but instead gradually to understand what he has become as his own fate and, hopefully, to accept it. But also with regard to the archetypal forms with which our experience of childhood is bound up, it remains generally true that the more archetypal they are, the further removed they are from consciousness. Thus, especially in the beginning stages of therapy, we often encounter large numbers of archetypal dream images.

Displacement and archetypal over-elevation of one's childhood experiences also serve to protect a weak ego from invasion by overwhelming emotions. Only with increasing ego strength can the individual gradually afford to come into contact with his early experiences and to permit them and their often distressing affects to surface.

2. If dreams themselves do not address childhood experiences directly, why is it so important to devote time and attention to one's childhood in analysis?

For Freud the analysis of childhood meant discovering the true state of affairs; causality, the search for causes, was for him strongly associated with the principle of truth. The image of the analyst in early psychoanalysis was closely linked to the image of the detective. This also held true for Jung in the early stages. The point of analysis was to discover past mistakes and make use of these findings to contribute to the analysand's recovery. In the two or three generations since the discoveries of Freud and Jung, the image of the analyst has changed. Today it includes more compassionate, feminine attitudes in the place of patriarchal ones. Analysts have distanced themselves somewhat from equating the finding of truth with healing, the belief that discovering the facts equals a change in consciousness. They no longer take the search for causes so absolutely, not least because of their awareness that the causes cannot always be found. This is particularly true for the analytical psychology of Jung, for which the personal aspect of a life story represents only one side of the truth, the other side being based in a transpersonal, universal human unconscious.

Examination of one's childhood is nonetheless extremely important in many cases, such as Bernhard's. It is of fundamental importance because the emotional apparatus of the child one once was is the same as that of today's adult, and it is precisely these feelings that unconsciously influence the adult's actions, often unfavorably. Even though the adult differentiates himself intellectually from his parents, he often behaves as though he were still a child and projects his parent complex onto other people and elements of his situation. For example, Bernhard saw a destructive father in every authority figure and also unconsciously saw institutions as big fathers whose impersonal impact would be that of a repressive father. This had an extremely detrimental effect on his life, since he never was able to establish an unburdened relationship with an authority figure that let him exist in his own right. As a result, he rebelled and was unable to move in the direction of adulthood. It was thus essential for him to learn to differentiate between past and present and to distinguish between his own father and father figures in the world around him. Also important was the insight that emotions such as rage, helplessness, anxiety, and sadness were aimed at definite people, mostly his parents as they were during his childhood. One has to get through the stage of blaming one's parents so as to arrive at an unburdened relationship to father and mother. In addition, for the sake of the wholeness of the personality, it is essential to integrate and work more freely with the various emotions one has repressed one's whole life long out of consideration for family beliefs. If one's parent complex and childhood are not analyzed, one cannot adequately deal with one's own emotions, especially the so-called negative ones. For example, rage either overruns a person or he fears his own aggression to such an extent that he does not risk expressing it anymore, and thus an important emotional quality becomes blocked by aggression.

Rediscovering our childhood is important, in my opinion, not so much because it reveals the causes that shape our behavior as because it enables us to reexperience and integrate the affectivity linked up with our childhood. Thus we rediscover more completely our sense of innocence and our sense of attunement to our own feelings.

Furthermore, I believe it is important that we not only know our own history but also understand it, for three reasons. First, if we understand how we developed, we begin to understand our parents and their mistakes (for, after all, all parents make mistakes). Gods become human beings and tolerance makes its appearance. Second, by working through our childhood history, we can find an anchor in time, in the past. And third, understanding our history leads to understanding of, and tolerance for, our own inconsistencies and our complexes. The person who understands "how it all came about" develops the acceptance of and empathy for himself that are so necessary for life.

Developing this kind of sympathy was important for Bernhard because he frequently treated himself negatively, just as others had once treated him, scolding himself and tearing himself to shreds. At the end of his dream about the iron fist that brutally held him back, a little girl appeared, crying. He says in the dream: "For the first time she has heard her own tale of woe"— that is, her own life story. This part of the dream anticipated the attitude of greater tolerance and compassion toward himself that was gradually appearing in Bernhard's consciousness. It is typical that this attitude is represented by a girl. The feminine, compassionate side of Bernhard had been repressed. Having had constantly to repress his fear, he had lost the habit of feeling, of relating to his own feelings and, within limits, experiencing compassion toward himself. Instead of always berating himself, it was important for him gradually to develop the ability—symbolized by the crying child—to genuinely mourn for himself and his childhood so as to free himself to relate to the rest of the business of life.

3. How does one get at childhood experiences in analysis when even dreams, at least at the beginning of analysis, do not address these experiences directly—and to further complicate things, when one's memory is inadequate and biased and often hides behind various masks?

We cannot approach our childhood history in analysis only through questioning and dreams. What else can we do to extend our knowledge and help the analysand to increase his self-understanding? When someone like Bernhard perceives his environment unconsciously and illusorily as a despotic father and sees policemen, military men, and teachers everywhere, most likely he also views his analyst in this way. This was in fact true with Bernhard and me; I also became his "father" as his childhood experiences repeated themselves in the analysis. "Transference" is the technical term for this process in which the analysand transfers the image of his parents onto the analyst and experiences himself once again as the child he once was. The transference also naturally influences the analyst, who sometimes, as in the case of Bernhard's analysis, feels corresponding father reactions in herself. These reactions can be a matter of the analyst's own complexes, but they can also be linked to the analysand, who is unconsciously determined to get the analyst to react like his father. This inner reaction of the analyst to the analysand is called countertransference. By paying particular attention to the interaction between the analysand and the analyst, we learn much that is important about the childhood of the analysand.[2] The following is an example.

Quite soon after the beginning of analysis, Bernhard described a dream about a woman working at a newsstand who monitored everything going on around her. He felt threatened by her. He felt he was under her critical scrutiny, as he had been under his father's. In this dream he was experiencing himself as a child who could not be trusted and had to be watched. It is easy to see that this was a transference dream. Probably Bernhard experienced me as someone who wanted to scrutinize everything and check up on his every action. After having this explained, Bernhard reacted with relief, and our interaction became more relaxed. His perception of me as someone checking up on him was then related to the underlying childhood experience. It turned out that Bernhard had been exposed to excessive control by his parents. Childhood memories such as those I have described earlier came up and could be discussed. The corresponding feelings, of which he was increasingly aware, were also revived. These feelings had initially been directed toward his parents; these feelings had been denied legitimate expression. The intensity with which he currently was reacting to the authority figures around him was not really justified by the situation. Through various similar instances of dealing with his transference, not only were his memories lured out of hiding, but Bernhard also developed a growing ability to distinguish the present from the past and was gradually able to withdraw his immense father projection from the people he was currently relating to.

Gradually Bernhard began to understand himself and his complexes better and was also able to connect them with his childhood experiences. A further stage related to the child motif in his dreams was that Bernhard himself appeared increasingly in his dreams as the controlled and manipulated child he had been. The theme freed itself gradually from displacement onto other people and began to implicate the dreamer himself. Here is an example of a dream that clearly shows the transition from "some" child to Bernhard himself:

> A little boy finds himself in an elevator. His father is cruel and torments him by slowing down and then accelerating the elevator from outside, thus preventing the boy from getting out. I am the boy. I have the terrible feeling of being completely at his mercy. Yet in time I succeed on my own in escaping from the elevator.

In the statement "I am the boy," the dream indicates a decisive change in consciousness, which shows that Bernhard had now established a relationship with the former child in himself. In addition, the paternal element now increasingly took the form of his personal father. Along with this came changes in the father image, which were representative of Bernhard's experiences and could be evaluated as important stages in his confrontation with the father problem. First, a differentiation between the father and the archetype of the father became clearly recognizable. When the father image remains undifferentiated from the archetype underlying it, it acquires too much emotional significance, far out of proportion with the actual influence of the personal father. Wherever the archetypal element appears, there is the danger of overwhelming the ego (in a positive as well as a negative sense) and robbing it of its standpoint. The archetype is always inhuman and stereotypic, and thus far exceeds the human measure. When, as in Bernhard's case, the perception of the personal father is confused with the archetypal image, an intensity and explosive force are built up in the unconscious for which the ego is hardly a match. The next dream instructed Bernhard to reflect on the ways in which he experienced his father as overpowering.

> I am at home at my parents' house. It is evening, almost dark. I am sitting with my father in the study chatting with him. He tells me a joke, but I am not enthusiastic. I try to explain to

> him that I have two sides in me: one that strives for that which
> is pure, another that obeys the dark side, lust, pure desire.
> Then I tell him about a dream in which Dracula appeared to
> me. At that moment my father bends over me and is Dracula.
> I flee in panic-stricken terror into my parents' bedroom.

When the father bends over the dreamer, he appears combined
with the blood-sucking vampire Dracula of horror-film fame. This
horror, this terrible destructive power, conceals the personal father. When mothers and fathers appear as so excessively powerful in the experience of their children, the personal parent
image has been contaminated with archetypal images and thus is
connected with powerful forces. Separating the parents as people
from the archetypal exaggerations of them is a decisive step in the
differentiation of consciousness. In relation to the archetypal father, for example, one is always a child. But when the personal
father appears, the possibility exists of growing out of the filial
role and establishing a partnerlike relationship with the father.

An additional change in Bernhard's work on this problem was
the increasing appearance of his father as a *personal* father in his
dreams. They depicted him unvarnished and clearly reflected
Bernhard's childhood attitude toward him. The following two
dreams are examples.

> I am traveling with my father in a car. There is heavy traffic.
> I am frigid with fear, but Father doesn't understand me.
>
> While skiing, I approach a fork in the path. I no longer have
> any skis. I continue on through the snow with my girlfriend.
> My mother comes up to us to say good-bye. Then a group of
> people comes, my father among them. He looks at me in such
> a way that I know I have to go to him; I submit to the pressure
> of his eyes even though I resist it.

In connection with these and many similar dreams, Bernhard
began to feel strongly the rage against his father that he had
previously repressed. There followed a period in which he saw
only the negative side of his father, and an intense inner emotional confrontation with his father began. During this time he
experienced rage and helplessness, but also mourning. In his
mourning he became aware of the excessive demands he made

on his father, and little by little he could see things in relative terms. His father was seen more and more as a person reduced to human size and finally even appeared in the dreams in a positive form. This sudden appearance of positive qualities made possible a compensatory balancing of the one-sidedly negative father image. Two dreams show the change:

> In the family circle. There is a different feeling. Father talks to my sister, asking her for something, but it is actually a demand. I speak to him about it. He reacts, stunned that I dare to do this. But then he is surprisingly open.

> I find myself with a group of people, including my father and many other people. We are looking for a place outside on the lake. It is still quite cool, so we are on the lookout for a place to sit, and we discover a little bench right on the lake. Yet we have to use a kind of rope ladder to get down to it. Everyone climbs down, only I stay above because I am afraid. Father encourages me by saying that it isn't dangerous. Still I am afraid of the ladder, to which crabs are clinging. But I finally risk it anyway. Father continues to encourage me, and I reach the ground without difficulty.

In both dreams the father appears friendly and gives time and attention to his son; in this respect, the father image has become positive.

Now came another step in the process. In the course of his development, Bernhard had also internalized—or introjected—his father, and he had to realize now that he often acted just like his father. This theme appeared in his dreams, once again in connection with the motif of the child:

> Next to a man is a little girl, whom I send, God knows why, into the street. I have the feeling that I am really pushing her out there. In the sky appears a gigantic cloud in the form of Death. It approaches the child, whom I have apparently sent to her death. The child now appears in the sky carrying a glowing red sphere. I am afraid that Death could come take me now too. My girlfriend is near me, and I seek out her protection. "R——," I say, "I am so afraid, so terribly afraid."

In this dream Bernhard sends the little girl out into traffic and ultimately to her death. He has become just as mortally threatening as his father. Bernhard at first understood the girl to be his own feeling side, which he expected too much of and sent out into "traffic," or society, too quickly. Actually Bernhard seldom allowed himself to simply observe his feelings impartially and without fear. He mostly ignored them and demanded conformity to collective values and norms from himself. In this way he completely neglected himself, destroying the sensitive side of his nature. The importance of the little girl is shown in the red sphere that she holds in her hands. The sphere can be understood as a symbol of the Self, which makes up the innermost aspect of one's individual ground of being. By ignoring his own feelings—and this is the way Bernhard understood the dream's message—he mortally threatened the most valuable part of himself, his Self. The child in the dream stands not only for the child that Bernhard once was but also for his potential, his future possibilities. The dream instructed him to attend to them, to behave toward them as a good father; Bernhard recognized this lesson through the analysis of the dream.

A person who is integrating his childhood and tries to observe his own inner child, which is often the carrier of the Self, experiences a change in the way he relates to the children in dreams over a period of time. Bernhard, who, like his father, in his dreams frequently became angry at children and treated them unfairly, began to change the way he behaved toward them. Also, more people appeared in his dreams who treated children well, as in the following:

> A mother yells at her child. The ball has rolled somewhat too far for him. My girlfriend brings the ball to the child and tells him that nothing so terrible has happened.

In this dream his girlfriend is not only Bernhard's companion but also represents his own kindly side, which was able to behave in a measured and compassionate way toward natural and childlike manifestations. In another dream Bernhard stood up for a happy, noisy crowd of children and opposed the negative father attitude that had been handed down to him:

> I am walking through a wooded area, a really relaxing coun-
> tryside. Then along comes a pack of small schoolchildren
> who are happy to be able to romp about freely. An older
> pedestrian gets angry about their boisterousness. Isn't there
> any place anymore where a person can find some peace and
> quiet? I feel I have to express myself too and take the chil-
> dren's side. I let him know that there are worse noises than
> children shouting—power saws, for example.

In the course of analysis Bernhard developed greater autonomy; he gradually grew out of the son or child attitude and was
able to take his place in groups of fathers without viewing them
as persecuting and critical, controlling figures. Analysis of his
childhood—assimilation of his experiences with his father and
the fatherly side of his mother—enabled him to take his parents
off the tyrant or god pedestal and to see them as people with
their own life stories. Becoming aware of his own inner child
encouraged his tolerance and compassion for himself, led him
into the process of mourning for the childhood he had been
deprived of, and gave him the opportunity to relate to his own
inner child as a symbol of depth of feeling and thus let himself
live his life more naturally and spontaneously.

The following dream was a sign to Bernhard that he was no
longer a child but could and should be an adult:

> People are arguing about who has to carry a heavy sack. The
> quarreling strikes me as just too stupid, so I begin to lift the
> heavy sack onto my shoulders. Someone gives me instruc-
> tions on how best to handle the sack without hurting myself.
> I almost reach my limits in lifting the sack, but in the end I
> am able to do it. My parents really wanted to prevent me from
> carrying out my intention.

Bernhard experienced the inner and outer parents as life-
inhibiting. In the dream he asserted himself and took on the full
burden of responsibility for his own life. What appeared here in
the dream as a prefiguration of future potential was later man-
ifested in the outer actions of becoming a family man and a
competent professional. From a person whose enjoyment of life
was threatened and whose inner child was not permitted to live,

Bernhard increasingly became a person who enjoyed life and who, as was said in one of his dreams, "suddenly wanted to live."

Thus far, this chapter has implicitly raised several questions that could be meaningful to anyone who is working with his or her own inner child and its psychology. These are the questions that each person can ask about his or her own dreams:

- How do I appear in my dreams, as a child or as an adult?
- What are the children in my dreams up to?
- How do I treat children in dreams?
- How do other dream figures treat them?
- How do parents and other authority figures appear?

These and similar questions offer a way to become better acquainted with the inner child and to enter into relationship with it.

THE CHILD AS SACRIFICIAL VICTIM

In this section I shall describe how children frequently fall prey to the unconscious fantasies of their parents. Whereas in the discussion of Bernhard's analysis, the focus was on the personal history of the analysand, I intend now to look at childhood from the historical-mythological perspective. This will show that even the actions and modes of expression of modern people are linked to eternal human archetypal patterns. While the form of these patterns is endlessly variable, their contents remain the same.

Child sacrifice was widespread in earlier times. This may well be explained by children's unbroken young strength, which is capable of warding off evil and harmful forces. A quick look at a number of child-sacrifice practices may give us an understanding of this theme. Formerly, it was customary to sacrifice the most powerful members of a society—kings and nobles—to ensure future good fortune for a people. The Swedes, for example, sacrificed their king Olaf to the god Odin. Later, child sacrifice came about as a substitute for these royal sacrifices. The closest to the original custom was sacrifice of the king's son; later, any child was used. But primarily children were sacrificed for the preservation of dwindling physical strength. It is said of the Swedish king Aun that, to stop the aging process, he had one of his ten sons sacrificed to Odin every ninth year. Sacrificing nine sons in this way, he is supposed to have survived beyond the normal life expectancy. However, when he wanted to sacrifice the tenth son, the people refused, and even King Aun had to suffer death.

Children were also sacrificed for magical purposes. Giles de Laval, an alchemist, informs us that, as an initial gesture to start things off right, he offered up the heart, hand, and blood of a child to the demon who was to help him make gold. In German superstition, we often find mention of a child being promised to a heavenly or demonic power even before its birth. Reflections of this are found in many fairy tales: in "The Virgin Mary's Child," the child is promised to the Virgin Mary, and in "The Handless Maiden,"[3] a miller gives his daughter to an old man who later turns out to be the Devil. Last, we might mention the use of children as a sacrifice at the time of building a new house. To protect houses and their future inhabitants from harmful magic, living children were sometimes built into the walls. Particular emphasis was placed on keeping them in a good mood, so they were given, for instance, a roll or a slice of bread with gravy.[4]

And what of the situation today? Modern societies no longer carry out ritual child sacrifices, yet, it may be asked, do we not simply do the same thing more subtly and unconsciously? When we consider that probably all parents have more or less conscious fantasies about their children and recognize that such fantasies sometimes serve the satisfaction of an unconscious desire rather than the happiness of the child, we cannot overlook the thought that even today there is still a tendency to "sacrifice" children. Viewed practically, this can mean that a father or mother hopes to fulfill his or her own longings through the child. For example, a son might be made to live out the hidden ambitions of his mother or a daughter to achieve all the social advancement that the father failed to achieve in his own life. The variations are innumerable. If the secret intentions of the father or mother coincide with the talents of the child, it might turn out all right. But if the child does not have the necessary abilities, he runs into difficulties. He may be pushed into a state of rebellion that he cannot find his way out of or give up what he is really suited for in complying all too willingly with his parents' wishes. Unfortunately, even small children and infants are frequently related to by parents as possessions. The roles are reversed in that a father or mother then expects the child to display the qualities of an ideal parent, especially unlimited availability (the child obeys to the letter) and great flexibility (the child has to put up with every mood of the parents).

In all these cases the child is narcissistically owned, which means that the mother or father binds the child to him- or herself in self-love, and uses the child for egotistical purposes. The parents' self-love is served by being able to show off a well-bred, studious, and extremely polite child. In narcissistic possession the parents view their children as property that they can shape and dispose of without any consideration for the children's feelings. They may completely disregard the fact that the child has its own natural abilities, whose development is a foremost parental duty. Children used in this way become, to a certain degree, extensions of their parents and are under pressure to fulfill the parents' expectations of them at any cost. An important and relatively frequently observed variant of the narcissistic use of children appears when parents take out on the child their grudges against their own parents. To take a simple example, a mother may display excessive aggression toward her child. This aggression may, however unconsciously, be intended for the father toward whom she was never allowed to express rage. The child, who is available and weak (unlike the father, who was omnipotent and powerful), becomes a safe object on which to take out her aggression.

Children used in this way really become the sacrificial victims of their parents. The gods to whom they are sacrificed are psychological forces of which the parents are, as a rule, unaware.

The modern variant of child sacrifice can be observed in the story of Peter. The only child of quite affluent parents, Peter had a lonely childhood. His parents devoted all of their energy to a thriving business and could not look after the small boy much. In addition, Peter's mother did not look kindly on contact with the children in the community and prevented it whenever possible. Without siblings and surrounded almost exclusively by adults, he hardly experienced a happy childhood. Peter remembered that his mother often urged him to behave like a little "gentleman"; that was the highest praise that he could receive. Photographs show him as a well-mannered, frail boy with a fearful, tentative expression on his face.

When Peter was eleven, his father died quite suddenly. Thereafter he fell under the domineering influence of his mother even more. She saw him as heir to the business and started to mold and educate him accordingly.

Peter did not have a clear memory of his childhood; in particular, he had hardly any recollection at all of his father's death and the time before this tragic event. Specific details were recalled vaguely but without feeling. The gaps in his memory were conspicuous and called for an explanation. In the course of the analysis it turned out that Peter had probably experienced too little mirroring from his mother. In other words, his needs had not been given enough time and attention. As a child who had been used to fulfill the wishes of his parents, his own makeup and potential were neglected, and despite the best external care and the constant presence of his parents, Peter was an emotionally abandoned child.[5] A person who was emotionally abandoned as a child and whose needs were given too little time and attention knows himself poorly and has little connection to his own inner process. His self-awareness is seriously disturbed. When everything on the child's mind seems unimportant to the parents and is not seen by them, then the child gradually stops noticing his own needs and falls into a kind of self-alienation. This happened to Peter and was a major reason for his inability to remember his childhood. Another obvious reason was his father's death. Children who suffer the early loss of a parent and whose mourning is made impossible by various specious considerations pass over the death as though nothing happened, and later the death and the events surrounding it are almost completely erased from memory.[6] This could be another explanation for the gaps in Peter's memory.

The deficient perception of him by his parents, the early death of his father, and the intensified influence of his mother exposed Peter to an exceptionally great extent to narcissistic possession by his mother. The idea that he was intended to take over the business put him under pressure and sensitized him to expectations related to this.

Among Peter's few memories, one stood out particularly. Once, he recounted, he set a fire behind a gas station near the family business. He had wanted to burn the business down. From this event it can be deduced that Peter probably felt rage toward his parents and aversion to having been sacrificed on the altar of family tradition.

A picture Peter painted and a meaningful dream unmistakably point to this sacrificial role. An impression of the painting and its atmosphere is given in the accompanying sketch (fig. 3).

In a castle courtyard, surrounded by high walls and soaring towers, stands a small boy holding an oversized sword. The boy's isolation and loneliness are obvious; just as evident is the pressure under which he appears to stand. The towers, indeed the whole castle construction, can be understood as an indirect symbol of the business and the great expectations that towered over him. As the little hero, Peter stands in the middle, the heavy sword raised high. It is clearly, then, a hero fantasy that was projected onto him. This hero fantasy was the unconscious power complex to which he was sacrificed by his mother. The sword, the mark of the hero, is red in the original painting, and this symbolic color shows the great extent to which heroism possessed the boy's life energy. The mother (and surely the father as well) used the boy and possessed him narcissistically through a fantasy that actually belonged to her psyche and that *she* should have lived out rather than delegating it to the child.

FIGURE 3
A sketch of Peter's painting.

The pronounced disproportionality between the largeness of the sword and the smallness of the boy indicates the highly excessive demand that Peter must have unconsciously felt as a child and carried into adulthood. Too great a task had been imposed on him. This to a great extent explains the severe feelings of inadequacy that he continued to suffer from as an adult.

Peter's dream confirmed this picture of narcissistic possession, adding more features to it. The dream went like this:

> I am about five and chained to my mother's leg. This also serves to support my mother. We go into a restaurant. There the chain is briefly unlocked so that I can drink a glass of milk. My mother is extremely proud that she is able to provide me with the best teachers of Indian wisdom, yogis. In addition she is full of pride about my cleverness and wisdom. Still, in the dream I think about wanting to use what my mother gives me for my own purposes rather than hers.

Peter dreamed of himself as a child, which for one thing was a reference to his experience in childhood and, for another, made clear that even though he was now an adult, he was sometimes still shackled to his mother. The dream also indicates that his being chained also provided support for his mother. When parents bind their children to them excessively, they seldom do it for the well-being of the child alone, but rather also to support themselves. The mother as a concrete, external person and as a mother complex within him remained forces that turned his life into a sacrifice. While in his painting the hero fantasy stands out, the dream indicates that his mother also projected the fantasy of the wise man onto him. In this way, too, Peter's mother used him and unconsciously conveyed to him the message that he would be loved and could count on her pride in him only if he lived the life of a wise man for her. At the same time, a first attempt at differentiation appears in the dream. In the dream Peter at least wants to use what his mother has provided him with for himself. And indeed, he was able to accomplish this to a great extent in his life.

A discussion of Peter's mother's history made clear why this woman nurtured strong fantasies about a great man. As the offspring of a famous and powerful American family, she had come to Germany in her youth and married a man of Jewish descent there. The Second World War brought the couple great suffering. Her husband survived deportation but returned home from the concentration camp a broken man. When her only son was born, she unconsciously transferred her fantasies of lost greatness to him. They arose from the tradition of her family background and also drew nourishment from the fate of her husband, who was not able to regain his original energetic nature after the terrible war years.

Thus Peter had been made a sacrifice to his mother's fantasies of outstanding manliness and great wisdom. A long analysis was necessary to help Peter achieve release from his enchainment to his mother and be able to strive for his own self-fulfillment.

When I reflect on Peter and the fate of others similar to him, the Greek hero Achilles comes to mind. He was the son of King Peleus and the nymph Thetis. His divine mother wanted to make her son immortal and held him over a magic flame after his birth. Since previous children had already fallen victim to the flames, her husband Peleus was on the alert and was able to save Achilles at the last minute. He delivered his son to the centaur Chiron to educate him, and Chiron became Achilles' excellent teacher. Many parents behave like Thetis, and many also are the fathers who wish great things for their children. In this way the child is often victimized and his impulse to self-realization destroyed. When that happens, one can only hope that this child sacrificed to an unconscious psychological force may receive help from another parent and later find a master as wise as Chiron.

A Childhood Marked by Illness

The childhood of children who are ill is distinguished mostly by the inability to properly negotiate the developmental stages of the appropriate age group. The child might be confined to bed, for example, and unable to satisfy the impulse toward activity. Or he may be isolated in the hospital where he cannot be touched, embraced, or even stroked by parents or caretakers; and this happens at an age when physical affection is so terribly important, when the child finds security primarily in the tender, loving touch of his parents. Finally, sick children often have drastic experiences of separation. We know from widely conducted studies that such experiences have an extremely unfavorable effect on the emotional life of a child. This is true because separations are often experienced as a breaking off of all connection to the mother, or even as her death.[7]

The sick child has not been optimally equipped by Mother Nature and thus begins life under the sign of the archetypally constellated negative mother. When the negative mother comes into play at the archetypal level, the psyche is shaped by a negative mother complex. The child experiences several kinds of deficiencies. For one, the mother-child relationship is disturbed and the child does not receive enough growth-enhancing maternal care. The sick child, confined to bed or in the hospital, quite simply cannot elicit the same amount of mothering from the mother or caretaker as the healthy child can. In addition, it is not uncommon for the mother to be overburdened by the child's illness. Long, wakeful nights, constantly having to carry the child around, disturbed sleep, and the complaints of the sick child's siblings cause the mother to react irritably, unintentionally upsetting the child.

Another aspect is that a negative mother complex brings the experience of having no solid inner ground in oneself. The child becomes uncertain and inhibited and, as a result, cannot develop the trust in himself and the world that he urgently needs.

Finally, the mother complex leads to a certain untimely maturity. The child imitates adult behavior too early and becomes aware too soon of many things that other children do not yet have to think about. Children manifesting this early maturity give the impression of being understanding, reasonable, willing to adapt and ready to help—all, naturally, at the expense of their own naive childlike quality and innocent spontaneity. Guilt feelings also play a major role, for the child as well as for the parents. A sick child is simply more frustrated than a healthy one. In the early years of childhood, children internalize frustration as guilt; thus the so-called primary guilt feeling arises. For example, during hospitalization, the mother has to leave the child alone. For the child, this means withdrawal of love, which he interprets like this: "Mother doesn't love me; I am bad and it's my fault." On the other hand, the guilt feelings of the parents are based on their sense of failure. They know that the sick child has a hard lot and unjustly feel themselves to blame. This can interfere with their spontaneous affection for the child. A sick child is an endangered child, and in most cases parents do all that is humanly possible to prevent further harm. They often react overprotectively. As a result the child is oversupervised, oversheltered, and warned too often about possible dangers. This makes the child insecure and causes an additional weakening of his or her already low self-confidence.

These difficulties encountered by children with long-term or chronic illness is ultimately a matter of fate, a fact that should release parents from their guilt complex. Only rarely is there any blame to be laid. Failing to see this point can cause a childhood marked by illness to have consequences that last beyond the actual time of affliction and continue into adulthood. These consequences take the form of basic uncertainty and relationship problems, manifesting particularly as an abandonment complex. [8]

Every illness entails a sense of abandonment, whether for a short or long period. People who suffer from an abandonment complex try later to arrange their lives so that the agonizing feelings associated with it are no longer touched. I shall briefly describe two of the most typical patterns.

There are people who are conspicuous for their self-sufficiency. They appear self-reliant and independent and rarely enter into close relationships. Behind this facade is often an abandonment complex that can be controlled and held at bay by means of the mostly unconscious basic principle "I am sufficient unto myself and have no need of anyone else." The other pattern is a marked striving for fusion, or merging, in which an individual seeks to bind other people to himself and bring about a symbiotic attachment in the pattern of the mother-child relationship of early childhood. There is also a tendency here to try to make other people dependent on one and rope them into "service." By handling feelings of abandonment in this way, the person succeeds in maintaining the illusion of constantly having other people at his disposal and not being alone. Both these ways of coping with abandonment can coexist in the same person.

One young woman, whom I shall call Monica, had a childhood entirely overshadowed by illness. Soon after her birth the doctors noticed a hip dislocation. At two months, Monica was put in a plaster cast that enclosed her abdomen and legs, greatly restricting her freedom of movement. To begin with, she could not move about; later she was unable to crawl or walk. For the most part she had to be carried. The cast had to be replaced every six weeks because of her growth; the result was that Monica could spend only six weeks at home before once again having to spend ten days in the hospital. This continued until well past her second birthday, thus lasting well over two years. Finally,

Monica had to have an operation. During the first years of her life the child was often in ill health. Head colds, flus, and angina occurred frequently, so that she continued to require nursing even at home. These are the years during which a child masters her surroundings, begins to crawl and then walk, struggles away from her mother, and as a rule is extremely active. All of this was out of the question for Monica. Hospital stays occurring in regular succession must have had a traumatic effect on her. While she was in the hospital, she could hardly have visitors. In those days hospitals did not allow parents to visit their children regularly as they do now, and they had to be content with seeing Monica once a week through a glass panel.

After these years of almost complete lack of movement, Monica's hip dislocation improved to the point where she was able to lead a normal life without a cumbersome cast or disruptive hospital stays. Her health did continue to leave much to be desired until about her eighth year. All the same, she developed satisfactorily, fitting into her kindergarten and primary school situations without problem. She was a gifted child in every respect and got through school easily. Monica's extraordinary musical talent became apparent early on and was appropriately encouraged. After graduating from high school, she began training as a physical therapist, a profession that was just getting started at the time. She successfully completed this training and accepted a job at a clinic for handicapped children.

Years later she decided to go into analysis. She wanted to know herself better, broaden her qualifications as a therapist, and gain insight into her disturbing tendency toward symbiotic relationships.

At first the analysis proceeded smoothly. We dealt with Monica's life history, her relationship problems, and her dreams. Then our work together began to falter, and one day Monica came to me and said that she had felt alone in the last session and had been unhappy and frustrated. I was glad that she had been able to say this to me and also that the abandonment complex that I assumed because of the nature of her childhood had appeared in the transference and thus had a chance of being understood and worked through.

Naturally Monica had told me about her childhood, mentioning the difficult years of restricted movement. Because of her therapeutic training she knew the possible consequences of such a serious handicap. But knowing about it does not bring healing of the wounds. Often analysands say, "What good is it to know what happened in my childhood? This knowledge doesn't change a thing!" How right they are, for only when the negative experience associated with the frustrating events is activated in transference and experienced in relation to the therapist can it be worked through. When Monica said to me that she had felt abandoned by me, I had to assume that the decisive experience was beginning to play out between us. Again, knowledge alone does not bring change; only reexperiencing the affective memory—the memory that evokes the emotion bound up with it—in the analytical setting offers hope of working through one's childhood and thus healing its wounds.

Usually it takes some time before the analysand ventures into transference. This is because transference involves reliving painful feelings of the past. Further, the analysand does not know how the analyst will handle these feelings and justifiably protects herself from transference. In Monica's case, for example, it could be assumed that in the hospital her pain of separation, homesickness, and sense of abandonment were not dealt with appropriately because this would have placed too great a demand on the nursing staff. How could the child in Monica know whether she would find in me an understanding person if she let her old feelings out in the transference?

A few months before the session in which she said that I had left her alone, Monica had had a quite vivid dream:

> I am a small child, about two years old. I am standing alone in a house under construction. I call for my mother repeatedly. In doing this I have the feeling that if I am not heard, I also will not exist. Then I stop crying out, but I am quite afraid, afraid of going crazy. In the dream I also sense—now as an adult again—that I dare not get involved with these

feelings; they are too dangerous. I have the feeling that I really have to wake up because I shouldn't venture into these feelings on my own.

This dream depicted Monica's experience of abandonment. In addition, it made her aware of a real experience in its total reality, as it had been felt at the time.

This dream message is exemplary of the experience of children. The statement that Monica would not exist if she went unheard sums up the reality of the small child. The small child's feeling of existence is dependent on being sufficiently seen and heard, on being adequately perceived in all her expressions. We call the ability of the mother or caretaker to respond in this way the maternal mirroring function.[9] In mirroring the child optimally, the mother lays the indispensable foundation of the child's sense of identity. For each of us our sense of identity depends on having been adequately seen and acknowledged as children. Monica's dream expressed this reality in succinct fashion: if I am not heard, I will not exist. That is the child's experience of abandonment. What counts here is not the concrete fact of not being heard, but rather that the child who is heard or seen has the sense of existing, and the child who is not heard or seen experiences an anxiety in which, according to her own subjective perception, she ceases to exist. This anxiety is called disintegration anxiety; it is the fear of falling apart or disintegrating and falling into a bottomless void. I concluded on the basis of the dream that this is the kind of fear and feelings of abandonment that Monica had experienced.

The dream also warned that it was too dangerous to get involved in these emotions. It seemed to me at the time that the dream was right. Only when trust in the analyst has grown to a critical point can the analysand allow herself to reexperience such disturbing feelings. Only when she is sure that she will not be left alone with these feelings can she risk sharing them with the analyst. But since the experience of most of the person's life is one in which these feelings have never been heeded, it is an enormously courageous step to let these feelings come up in analysis. On the basis of Monica's childhood history and the terrible experience depicted in this dream, an explanation for her symbiotic tendencies could also be found. Whenever she got to know a partner, she became extremely close to him. Unfortunately, she repeatedly encountered men who would not tolerate bonding and who kept their distance, provoking a sense of helplessness and disappointment in Monica, who had been fighting to keep her feelings of abandonment concealed behind symbiotic tendencies.

The call-for-help dream also had diagnostic value and appeared to me to illustrate Monica's primary complex. In contrast to clinical diagnosis, which involves clear-cut ailments such as depression or compulsive neurosis, such a dream can be described as complex-diagnostic. In my view, a dream acquires such a status when it provides the analyst with a clue to the central complex formative of the personality—in other words, when the analyst has an "Aha!" experience in connection with the dream. This is always more than an intellectual insight; it is based on an emotional reaction. The criterion for a complex-diagnostic dream is the analyst's being emotionally affected; this cannot be a matter of purely mental considerations. Such a diagnostic dream opens up the problem of the analysand to the analyst in one stroke, making it clear to him and giving him the feeling of understanding it. But the experience of emotional understanding is not limited to the analyst; as a rule, the analysand is also deeply affected. I would also designate a complex-diagnostic dream as an initial dream of understanding, in that it gives the analyst the feeling that all the information that has poured in up to this point has suddenly taken on meaning and revealed a pattern.

The criterion for deciding whether a dream is diagnostic in this sense is based more on emotions than on objective criteria that could be applied to any number of other dreams. Since it arises on the emotional level, it is not something that can be applied generally. The most that could be said is that if the analyst has this experience in connection with another dream, then the possibility that that dream, too, has diagnostic value should not be ruled out. The complex-diagnostic dream cannot be compared to a medical diagnosis. When a patient has appendicitis, one doctor can determine this and another confirm it. In analytical work, circumstances are somewhat different. First, the complex diagnosis in psychological work is dependent on the quite specific constellation between a particular analysand and a particular analyst; and, second, this diagnosis changes in the course of analysis. When I conclude that the abandonment complex is Monica's central complex, this means that this is the perspective that enables me to work well with her, which helps me to understand her. This would not necessarily be the diagnosis of another analyst. It is quite possible that in the interaction between Monica and another analyst, another central complex could be constellated, which would be the appropriate one for that analysis. With these reservations and appropriate caution, we may permit ourselves to speak of the complex-diagnostic value of a dream. Such a dream can help greatly to make childhood events understandable.

Having made these general observations, let us return now to Monica's dreams. They later supported the theme Monica had introduced—the abandonment situation appeared with increasing frequency. In the dream recounted below she went from one situation to another in which she was rejected, left unheeded, abandoned. This dream clearly shows the way in which the experiences of childhood are fused with those of adulthood. Today and yesterday are not differentiated from one another. The child's feelings have continued on intact as part of the adult's self-understanding, and the ego does not know that it is now experiencing feelings which are no longer appropriate in the present. But this is how complexes work. Monica's abandonment complex was triggered by the slightest occasion resembling abandonment, and her whole way of experiencing was tinged with its quality. Where complexes are at work, reality is always distorted, perceived through the lenses of the complex. Monica had this dream:

> I go to a therapist. I am quite sad during the session and become sadder and sadder because I have lost two jewels. The therapist accepts my dream images and is quite inter-

ested, but she talks past me and does not notice my sadness. I go out and lie down in the waiting room. She comes out and tells me that I should paint the sea at G——. I would prefer that she give me her attention. She says I should come back in the afternoon. But then I have to go see Mrs. Asper, so that's okay.

Then I am at home. Someone has dug up my garden; everything is ruined. I lie in bed in the morning covered with blood and boils. I urgently need to go to a doctor. Then I meet U——, who has no time. After that I meet a doctor who is going to an appointment and also can make no time for me. I can't talk about my illness there either. Then a student wants to live with me and move into the front room. He is a very jolly person. I clap my hands over my head and think that this will not work out well. Then I am with Mrs. Asper again, at seven-thirty in the morning. She is still in her housecoat and says I am too early. She shows me her living room, full of ceramic figures. Here I cannot talk about my illness either. Then I am with her at one o'clock in the afternoon. She is quite stern with me and says I have to be more structured and give up my "trips."

Then I am going somewhere, and cumulus clouds are coming up out of the earth like smoke.

The main features of the dream quite clearly show that Monica is pushed aside by everyone; no one has time for her, and she cannot say anything about her illness. Her therapists (I and an imaginary second one) are talking past her. So even in the one place where she could legitimately count on help, no one is listening. In addition, she is unable to capture people's attention so she can tell them about her pain.

A further, more important aspect of the dream is that something is coming out: from her body in the form of blood and boils, and from the earth as clouds and smoke. Monica is brushed off and is unable to communicate what is on her mind; she experiences something coming out of the depths—of her body, of the earth.

In considering this dream, it was essential to talk about all the situations in detail so that Monica did not have the feeling that I was not paying enough attention to her during the session. Being unheeded and abandoned were the central feeling qualities of the dream that we had to attend to right away. Then we looked into situations outside of analysis in which Monica felt rejected. Finally we dealt in detail with her inability to talk about what was on her mind. More and more individual aspects of her abandonment traumas in childhood, which were represented in the dream as boils and clouds of smoke, arose in connection with the dream. In her childhood, she had not been able to talk about her pain at all; no one had noticed it or had time to relate to it. Thus the way to her childhood experience had been rediscovered, allowing Monica little by little to connect the complex feelings of abandonment with the past and to situate them where they belonged. The past and present began to separate, enabling Monica's ego to find a certain distance from the distressing feelings of the complex. This particular dream does not depict a child, but it is a typical dream in that it portrays the feelings of childhood mingled with adult experience and contains clear indications that something from inside—from the depths—is coming out, and thus it points to the past.

It would, however, have been counterproductive merely to make the analysand aware of her childhood, because this would have been to fail to take her current experience seriously; thus what she experienced in transference would have been reduced to referring to her childhood alone. It was important to discuss with Monica all the moments in which she felt rejected or insufficiently acknowledged by me. These had actually taken place and deserved to be brought to light. No therapist can, nor should, avoid these frustrations. It is the foremost therapeutic rule to take the analysand's experience seriously and share it with her. If this had not taken place, Monica and I would have repeated her childhood experience of abandonment, and this bad experience of the past might not have found its way into our dialogue.

Here is another of Monica's dreams, this one directly involving a child.

> I am dreaming about a sweet, alert blond child. She was inexperienced, alone. I met her playing at our neighbor's in W——. When the little girl's ball went over the fence, I got

it and in retrospect was amazed by my courage, because the
neighbor had several ferocious dogs. Then I take the child by
the hand because a car is coming. But the child is determined
to go into the street to stop the the car, which she regards as
an amusing plaything. I am startled, annoyed, and concerned
that the child has so little idea of the dangers of the street,
and I slap her, then immediately regret it.

Then I take the child home with me, and my mother agrees
to having the child stay overnight with us. I carry her around
the whole time and rock her to sleep as though she were my
own child. I have taken her into my heart, and she goes to
sleep, calm and secure with me.

Two things need to be emphasized in this dream. On the one
hand Monica relates to the child lovingly; on the other, she
shows little understanding and slaps her forcefully. And this is
how it actually was in reality: Monica had good contact with the
child in herself, for she radiated naturalness, curiosity, and
spontaneity, but she was capable at times of abruptly blocking
off these impulses without warning—as with the slap in the
dream—and silencing them. This came about mostly when she
noticed tendencies in herself that she viewed as socially unac-
ceptable, tendencies that, to use the imagery of the dream, did
not belong in traffic, meaning around people. These "shut-
downs" reflected the way the people to whom she related closely
in her childhood had responded to Monica's spontaneous impulses. In the hospital her impulses had not been taken into
account; there, people did not have the time necessary to give
her special attention. At home, where a loving atmosphere actually prevailed, there was generally still little empathy, and
Monica had to adapt too quickly without explanations. Even the
adult Monica impatiently demanded adaptiveness from herself
at the expense of her feelings and sensitivities; in other words,
she simply gave them a good "slap" without properly acknowledging them. Many people treat themselves this way and silence
the inner child and with it that function in themselves that most
purely expresses their genuine reactions.

The other aspect of the dream, Monica's loving treatment of
the child, goes together with many other dreams she had in

which she treated children respectfully and lovingly. These dreams had a compensatory nature, meaning that they balanced out the frustrating experiences of childhood by encouraging a much-needed positive inner mother-child relationship between Monica and the child within. These favorable dreams were connected to the archetype of the child. Beyond the personal unconscious that contains our history as we have actually lived it, the individual is always connected to the depth level of the psyche, which Jung called the collective unconscious.[10] He chose the term *collective* because every person is linked to the collective unconscious and takes part in its storehouse of predispositions and images. This level is fundamentally healthy and so tends to compensate for forbidden and neurotic behavior patterns. The child in Monica's dream is, to some extent, the healthy prototype of the child in general and compensates for the sick child of Monica's childhood. Monica's way of relating with her also linked her with the collective unconscious by connecting her with positive maternal potentialities.

Now let us take a look at one last child dream of Monica's:

> I come into a church that is laid out in the form of a cross in which the end of every leg forms an apse. I walk to the entrance on the west side and move forward. In the apse is a picture; men are in it and a—Jesus?—preaches the word of God. I don't like the picture, and I turn around and make my way toward the exit. Then I come to the apse opposite the picture. A baptismal font filled with water stands there. Beside it is likewise a picture: an impressionistic depiction of water. Up in the gallery is an organ; wonderful music is heard. A small, approximately two-year-old child is now being baptized. The child, although it is so young, is also old at the same time. It is quite clearly a holy child. I am a little fearful of the cold water on the child's account, but it is obvious that it cannot trouble him.

The dream shows the child clearly as a holy, divine child and thus expresses the child as archetype even more clearly than the previous dream. The divine child (which I discuss in detail in chapter 3) is a psychic model that mediates to the individual the idea of the comprehensive and transpersonal character of the child principle. Such a principle cannot be fully integrated; it exceeds the human dimension. When it appears in dreams, it points to something new and gently balances out old and rigid modes of experience and well-worn thinking patterns.

At the front of the church hangs a picture depicting men, one of whom is preaching the word of God. The picture displeases Monica, and she turns back to the entrance. In confrontation with her childhood, Monica became aware of dogmatic religious values, which she experienced as restrictive and antiquated. She found them too patriarchal and devoid of spirit. However, in the dream before Monica finally leaves the church, she comes upon the picture of water and the holy child being baptized, and she notices the beautiful organ music. Clearly here is life; here, too, is living water.

She dreamed this dream during a time of inner barrenness and great conflict. After the dream she felt miraculously changed in mood, invigorated and centered. She did not want to spoil the dream by talking about it too much and made it clear to me that I should not start interpreting it analytically. She was right about this and at the same time was taking seriously the dream message about being displeased by the powerfully worded preaching. I respected her request. Important about the dream was the lasting effect of the feelings experienced in it and the emotional change connected with it. In the emotional atmosphere conveyed by the dream, Monica felt whole, healed and unified. The child in dreams often stands for a completeness that can never be fully achieved and conveys experientially the feeling of personal unity.

An interesting process became apparent when I let Monica's dreams go through my mind—her dreams from the period when the abandonment complex was strongly constellated and Monica also felt the accompanying experience in the transference relationship with me. This process can be seen even just in the dreams included here. To the extent that Monica reexperienced her former frustrations and affective memories came to the surface, the healthy, cheerful, and divine child appeared as compensation. The path back into the neurosis-producing past at the same time also opened up the way forward through child symbols that mediated a sense of wholeness and orientation toward the future. The failures of the past were balanced by healing symbols; next to the sick child of her early life was placed a healthy one with whom Monica was, in her dreams and later also in waking life, in a good, loving relationship.

So-called reductive analysis, the confrontation with the past, is in my opinion closely linked to final analysis or synthetic analysis, that is, with future-oriented elements and their meaning. It seems to me that the feelings that are dredged up and revived in the search for causes lay the groundwork for the forward-striving and future-building impulses and symbols of the psyche.

2   The Child as a Symbol of Life

THE MORE DEEPLY I delved into the theme of the child and dreams, the clearer became the meaning of the child as a symbol of life in general. This general meaning, however, has various facets, discussed in the following two sections. First comes an examination of depression. There we see the child symbol in connection with the denial of life. In the second section, the child as a symbol of new beginning is discussed. Here, in connection with the three themes of the end of depression, midlife, and the child in the realm of death, we encounter the child as a symbol of life in its transformational aspects.

THE CHILD IN DEPRESSION

Scientists worldwide have noted a striking increase in depressive illness in the last decade. Depression appears to have become a characteristic illness of our times. Indeed our time is characterized by a loss of the ability to feel and a deemphasis of human relationships, and the decline of basic shared values in favor of faster technology, a consumer mentality, and the general hustle-bustle of modern life. The word *depression* comes from the Latin *deprimere*, which means "to press down." In fact, the depressed person is pressed down and experiences himself as dull, without feeling, and overcome by sadness. Depression is a pathological psychological disturbance in which the following triad of symptoms appears:

- Sadness of mood: The depressed person is melancholy, apathetic, and anxious, while at the same time sullen and irritable. He suffers from a loss of feeling and can no longer be happy about anything. Moreover, he feels discouraged and looks at everything pessimistically.

- Inhibited thought process: The depressed person's thinking is slowed and often limited to very specific negative ideas, which have to be thought over and over again in agonizing monotony. A distinct tendency toward brooding is evident. The sick person reproaches himself, complains that he does not satisfy anyone or anything, and shows a marked incapacity to make decisions.
- Psychomotor disturbances: Facial expression and gestures are slowed, and the person has little initiative; he tends to sit and brood, hardly moving. In a prevailing mood of anxiety, on the other hand, the impulse toward activity can be intensified. Then, driven and harried by inner unrest, he must yield to meaningless compulsive activities and occupations.

Accompanying these three main symptoms are a variety of bodily symptoms such as feelings of heaviness, loss of energy, and a feeling of pressure in the head, breast and heart, and stomach areas. Depressed people also complain of sleeplessness and disturbed sleep, lack of appetite, and back and joint pains. However, a specific medical cause for these complaints cannot be ascertained.

Roughly speaking, three types of depression can be distinguished. We speak of endogenous depressions when the major distress can probably be attributed to congenital metabolic abnormalities in the brain. Included among these are the more rare depressions that proceed on a double track in which strong moods of elation, or mania, appear in alternation with depressive states. To the somatogenic depressions belong those which can be attributed to a demonstrable physical illness: for example, head injuries due to accident or tumor, or illnesses resulting from infection or metabolic abnormalities.

To the so-called psychogenic depressions—and the following cases are examples of these—belong the types of depression that can be explained by psychological causes. Among them are the reactive depressions, which are reactions, for example, to a traumatic event such as the death of a loved one or loss of the ability to walk caused by an accident. Also part of this group are the neurotic depressions, which are usually caused by prolonged, unfavorable living conditions in childhood and which are kept alive by the continual appearance of these emotional events. With proper treatment, either by psychotherapy or medication, depressions can be eased and often even healed.[1]

What depression actually is, is a loss of all spirit and vitality, a loss of the feeling of being alive. Depressions not only determine waking life but also express themselves in dreams, often producing scenes involving death. I find the following dream of the German poet Isolde Kurz (1853–1944) exemplary of these. Although I do not know the dreamer and have no knowledge of her situation at that time, the dream seems to me to speak of a desolate and life-denying existence in the depressive state. Only at the end, through the appearance of the mother, is a positive change noticeable.

> Once in Forte I had a dream. The earth was desolate, silent, without warmth, without light, without a single green blade of grass or the sound of a bird. I was the last person on the frozen planet; on a sloping surface, I slide downward across the eternal snow between white snow walls, lonely as no one had ever been before. Even when another human being, whose face was unrecognizable to me, appeared, it did not affect my loneliness. In the completely white snowy sky, I saw a pale circular disk, the moon. I wanted to feel happy that it was still there; then it rolled up like a pancake and fell as white streamers of snow. "Now the moon has died too," I said hopelessly. Then in the snow wall to my left there opened a niche like a tabernacle. Out of it bent the upper body of a female figure—my mother! I awoke from the immensity of the shock.

If depression can be roughly defined as the cessation of all sense of life and vitality, can we then expect the child, as a symbol of life, to appear in the dreams of depressed people, to be present within the domain of depression? At the beginning of my preoccupation with this question, I recalled a famous depiction of melancholy (an old term for depression), titled *Melancholy I* (1514), by Albrecht Dürer (1471–1528), reproduced in figure 4. In this enigmatic picture, among many other symbols arranged around the deeply sad feminine figure with downcast eyes, a child appears. It is what is known as a putto, the figure of an infant boy, who is enthusiastically writing or engraving a wax tablet. Putti are playful, happy young beings, in love with life, who appear frequently, not only in antiquity but especially in paintings of the fifteenth and eighteenth centuries. In playful poses, they appear in the paintings of every genre of this period. Although never the main theme of the work, they are lovely, charming additions. As cherubs, they also adorn many altars and church decorations.

What does the putto in Dürer's *Melancholy I* mean? This question stuck with me, and a study of the relevant literature revealed it to have a historical-iconographic meaning (that is, one derived from seeing Dürer's picture as conditioned by its time and tradition), in which the putto is understood as a symbol of concrete, spontaneous action, in contrast to the passive attitude of the dejected, philosophizing main figure. I would say that Dürer was using the putto, who is carefree and unburdened by thought, to personify the active life and to place it in contrast to the feminine figure, who is realizing with deep pain that she has reached the limits of her thinking. The putto is thus activity without the work of thinking, and the seated figure is a symbol of melancholy, of thought without the possibility of action and involvement.[2] This interpretation, put forward by renowned researchers, made sense to me, and I attempted to develop the ideas further on the psychological level. Actually, there are depressive states in which every thought ends up in one and the same abortive pattern, which presents a stark and painful contrast to the kind of vitality and activity represented by the putto. The depressed person experiences this conflict quite consciously. It is an agonizing experience in which life and the sense of being alive have gotten lost and, occurring outside of this gloomy condition, are neither available nor experienceable.

I wondered whether such lively children as the putto in Dürer's print appear in the dreams of depressed people. In all the dreams of analysands and depressed people I know of, I

FIGURE 4
Melancholy I (1514), engraving by Albrecht Dürer. Private collection.

have not encountered such lively children. At a conscious level, when one is awake, the lighthearted putto is experienced as a painful contrast to the depressed state. In the unconscious, however, in dreams, dead children often appear who represent the cessation or death of everything living. The dead child in dreams thus becomes a symbol of life-denial, the negation of the will and the capacity to live.

A CASE HISTORY

Herbert's main problem can be outlined in a few words. Herbert had been chronically latently depressed as far back as he could remember and had always experienced himself as vaguely sad. When this experience gave way to a manifest depression, he began therapy. He was fifty years old at the time. His view of himself was strongly characterized by negativity. He was haunted by guilt feelings and, although he could still function, continually experienced himself as not capable of adequately coping with life. A dream that related to the very heart of these experiential difficulties had made an idelible impression on him. Although he had dreamed it months before beginning analysis, he was still beset by anxiety.

> I am with two other players at a table; we are playing cards. Behind me appears an older woman dressed in black and darkly veiled. I turn around and touch her. At this moment I dissolve and am absorbed by her.

Within Herbert's psyche was a force that could obliterate him: a darkly dressed old woman in relationship to whom he is clearly characterized as younger, as a son. With her dark dress and dark veil, this woman, who is not personally characterized, betokens what is called the negative Great Mother. As a dark figure and mother goddess, she threatens his ego and has the power to destroy his life.

The dream provides an accurate representation of his relationship to depression. The dream showed him an image that stood in stark contrast to his activity of playing cards in the dream.

Playing cards is a symbol of life and engagement with life, of a lighthearted engagement with life altogether. In this symbol we see life as an ongoing play between gain and loss. Herbert, in the dream, is engaged with life and is playing life's game wholeheartedly. From behind, from the shadow side, the woman approaches him; she is, if he comes into contact with her, a life-threatening omnipotence. Looking more closely, we can also see in her a personification of depression. She is a figure of great potency best characterized as "queen of the night," the phrase with which the poet C. F. Meyer described melancholy.

When Herbert told me this dream, I was pleased with the image, since it enabled me to point out to him that his psyche had established contact with his depressive states.

It was an image that might be able to help him to somewhat objectify the dark events of his life. To apply this dream practically, what had to be done was discuss the course of Herbert's life and childhood with regard to people with whom he had experienced this sense of obliteration. We also had to uncover all those situations in his current life which he surrendered without a fight to gloomy moods, giving up his autonomy in an unquestioning sonlike fashion.

In another area of his depression, Herbert repeatedly dreamed not only of himself as a son and a child—that is, in a position in no way corresponding to his situation as the father of a family and a minister—but also of other children. He dreamed a number of times of dead children who could not be brought back to life despite major efforts. Two such dreams may be cited:

We are on a frozen lake. Many people are there, many children too. A child who belongs to me but is not my son ends up under the ice, and people immediately initiate a rescue operation, but in vain; they cannot find the child. Later the lake is emptied of water and there is a large bulldozer there with which the child is being looked for, but even with this they cannot not find him. Then I see the legs of the child jutting out of the mire.

A child is near a pond. It sits in the water, then falls into the water, goes under, then sits up again. I watch him because

this could be dangerous. But before I can get ready, the child
ends up under water and—is dead.

Children are obviously under threat, but the dreamer is not to
blame. On the contrary, every conceivable effort is undertaken
to save the children, especially in the first dream. The children
in these dreams stand for Herbert's orientation toward the future, for his spontaneity and aliveness. These qualities are
threatened; they run the risk of becoming unconscious, of falling
into the water or ending up under the ice. The children are, in
other words, in danger of being reclaimed by the suprapersonal
negative mother. The children also stand for the youngster that
Herbert once was. In his childhood, joie de vivre and spontaneity had hardly been possible, because of his mother, whom he
experienced as strict, his rigid religious education, and the
difficult experiences of wartime, including hunger and constant
fear and distress.

Herbert was plagued by strong feelings of guilt. With his
exaggerated sense of responsibility, he even felt guilty for things
he could do nothing about. These dreams were extremely important, because they showed his depression in the image of an
event that could befall him through no action of his own, that
came over him through the working of forces beyond his control.
These images relieved him quite a bit and also periodically freed
him from the negative and tormenting thought that he was to
blame for his depression. In Herbert's case depression was a
part of his life, and he had to gradually recognize these episodes
as symbolically periods of bad weather during which life—and
the child, as a symbol of life in his dreams—appeared dead.

THE CHILD AS A SYMBOL OF NEW BEGINNING

When depression approaches its end, we speak of a clear-
ing-up phase; initiative appears again, the disposition bright-
ens, and the spirits of life gradually return. This process
seldom proceeds upward smoothly. The condition remains del-
icate, and good days can unexpectedly be superseded by bad
ones. In this situation, dream images change too; the new be-

ginning expresses itself in them, offering solace and confidence to the person who has been depressed and is still uncertain. It is not uncommon at this point for the child motif to crop up in dreams.

In the final phase of a depression, a woman named Irene dreamed that she had borne a child whom she was delighted with and kept with her all the time. But suddenly she noticed that she had lost sight of the child. She immediately began to look for her and finally found her in a pond in the garden, lying lifelessly in the shallow water. At first paralyzed with fright, Irene overcame this feeling and lifted the child out of the water—she was dead. A bottomless grief seized Irene, and she was compelled to look again and again at the child, at her face drained of all color and her eyes staring sightlessly into the distance. To Irene's great astonishment the child began to stir, opened her mouth and eyes, making contact with Irene, and began to talk. Life had returned, and the dead child was living again, behaving as she had before. The dreamer took the child in her arms and was deeply moved by this mystery.

In this dream the child appears as a symbol, an embodiment of life itself. Corresponding to the coming and going of depressive states in the final phase of depression, the child is seen as dead one moment, alive the next. During this time it often happened that the life Irene had recaptured suddenly disappeared again and darkness gained the upper hand. The deeply impressive dream occurrence left her with the lasting experience that life does not die, that vitality can prevail against all probability, can re-emerge out of the unconscious and resume as before. The course of depression, with its ups and downs, its changeability, appeared as something mysterious, coming and going as it pleased. This mysterious flow of events was intimately linked in the dream to the secret of life, a process of death and rebirth in which Irene participated, both in the dream and in her daily life.

Also from the final phase of Irene's depression came the following dreams. In them, too, the child appears as symbol of regained life and new begining.

I am expecting a child. It is pushing and is already visible. I feel the birth water running down my legs. I am afraid that the child could be dead. A woman is looking after me and wipes the water off. She says the child is alive and healthy. I walk to the post office nearby. But I cannot give birth there because too many mailmen are watching. Now I run up the church lane. Snow is on the ground. I stumble over a motorcycle. I enter the church. There Mrs. B. is rehearsing a play based on a fairy tale with her children. It is about Snow White. Mrs. B. has a full face and thick blond hair. She has the children well under control. I go behind the pulpit. There I can give birth.

In a room a pharaoh mummy is lying in state, with its brown leathery skin. To my astonishment I see that the mummy is breathing slightly through its sunken nose and that the chest is rising and falling a little. In front of the mummy stands a baby carriage with a newborn boy who has healthy brown skin. I am astonished by the newborn's vitality.

The first dream deals with a birth. The dreamer still does not know where she should give birth, and she also encounters many obstacles along the way. Yet the child forces its way into life: life prevails despite all obstacles and lack of preparation. Finally, in the church, behind the pulpit, the dreamer is able to give birth.

The fairy-tale play that is being rehearsed is about Snow White. Snow White's apparent death in a casket can be understood as life coming to a standstill, as depression. In the tale, a piece of a poisoned apple got stuck in Snow White's throat and she fell down as though dead, whereupon the dwarfs put her in a glass coffin so that they could continue to enjoy her beauty. The poisoned apple came from the stepmother-witch. The apple, a symbol of Eros, is poisoned, indicating that for the depressed person the positive, loving emotions are lost. They are poisoned, which means that the depressed person has been overcome by destructive thoughts and fallen into the realm of the mother of death. Snow White's coffin is made of glass, for when we are depressed, we experience the world as if through glass: the feeling of having no feelings holds us in its spell, and our relationships, in which one experienced so much feeling, now seem as if they are no longer real, no longer belong to us. We see the people to whom we relate most as though through glass: though we can perceive them and know things about them, we no longer experience them directly or experience ourselves in them.

In Irene's dream, the child is born behind the pulpit. The place of birth is a central, protected area of the church. We observe again and again that people who have gone through one or several depressions find their way to a religious orientation. It seems that this support is attained at times of greatest distress. The theologian Romano Guardini wrote in reference to this: "Precisely the highest values are the most endangered. The higher is never attained in the ordinary course of life. It is always paid for with inner turmoil and peril."[3] Kierkegaard, who was afflicted by depression all his life, believed that the distance from God that we experience in depression is precisely what we need to reach an enduring experience of God. He writes in one of his journals: "But as long as the suffering lasts, it is often terribly painful. Still, little by little with God's help, we learn to abide in the belief in God, even in the moment of suffering; or at least as quickly as possible to return to God, even though it seems as though He might have let us go for a short moment while we were suffering. Indeed, it has to be this way, because if we could have God completely present with us, we would not suffer at all."[4] (The theme of the religious dimension of depression will be further developed in chapter 3, "The Divine Child.")

Irene's second dream is linked by subject to her first dream. Whereas in the first dream, Snow White appeared and one was reminded of her apparent death in the glass coffin, in the second dream a mummy appears. To the dreamer's great astonishment, the mummy begins to breathe. Breath is experienced by the dreamer as a symbol of life, more precisely, it signifies invigorating energy and creative spirit. In the Book of Genesis (1:2, 7), God awakens the man he has created with His breath, which is the expression of the creative spirit. The dreamer experiences the cosmic principle first as breath and then as a child lying in the baby carriage in front of the mummy. Both symbols, breath and child, represent the experience of the recommencement of all life; their vividness accentuates the end of depression and offers hope to the soul.

This revival and new beginning—experienced as a private individual by these women in their dreams—has been an important theme for all humanity throughout the ages. Prophecies about a new era and a coming golden age are numerous. We think of the ancient Egyptian prophecies, the Jewish Apocalypse, and the Revelation of Saint John, but also of the prophecy of Isaiah about the prince of peace: "For there is a child born for us, a son given to us, and dominion is laid on his shoulders; and this is the name they give him: . . . Prince-of-Peace" (Isa. 9:6). In this connection the famous and enigmatic shepherds' song, the fourth Eclogue (40/42 B.C.) of Vergil, deserves mention. Here, too, a child appears who will redeem the earth "from eternal horror." It is said about this child: "The earth itself will spread joyful flowers, small gifts for you, dear boy, to adorn your cradle with a miraculous blessing of blossoms. Even the animals of the field will pay homage to you." This child, it continues, will initiate the golden age: ". . . there is no more toil; everything is like a fairyland. Thus fate wills it, whose workers, the Parcae, are spinning the threads of a new age according to eternal counsel, on their humming loom."[5] In the prophecies, the hope for salvation takes on form—a new age is awaited. For such an auspicious new beginning and the accompanying deliverance from earthly pain, the child has been used as a symbol worldwide from time immemorial.

The salvational hopes of entire peoples and societies, which in the symbol of the child see and long for the power that makes new, correspond in the individual psyche to those symbolic dream children characteristic of the final phases of depression. These children, too, herald an auspicious phase of life. They, too, can initiate a new feeling of being alive. They are ultimately the expression of life itself and can be considered manifestations of the eternal human collective unconscious. Indeed, we are all connected to this depth level of psychological life. Yet we can never fully integrate its contents. The symbol of the child therefore points to the new with solace and hope. Nevertheless, we cannot extract from this symbol the promise of a better and happier time. The child in the dream should never mislead us about the fact that we bear an "earthly remnant" (Goethe), and therefore the symbolic child in its significance as life energy can never be completely integrated.

MIDLIFE

An important contribution of Jung's depth psychology is its conceptualization of life as constantly renewing itself. Learning a profession, conquering a place in the world, founding a family, and integration into the life process altogether should not be regarded as the sole end of our life's work. Life continues and relentlessly demands new steps of adaptation and maturation. Just at the juncture between the first and second halves of life, a crisis sets in for many people. The middle period of one's life draws to a close, and each person must accept his or her own mortality. The ability to take this step requires extensive adjustment and fresh adaptation from the individual. The merciless thought that we ourselves have grown old needs to be assimilated. Previous life goals require new orientation; new values become important. We often do not willingly participate in this change. It brings problems; we experience a sense of directionlessness and sometimes even suffer emotional and physical illness. With the sense of the end, of death, a more precise essentialization of our personality becomes necessary. In this restructuring phase many people begin to reflect on things left undone that they feel they must do before it is too late.

In this situation of new psychological orientation it is not uncommon for people—especially women—to dream about children. They give birth to a child, are overjoyed about it, and once again experience the bliss of being able to call a little living being their own. These little dream children often have peculiarities: there are Tom Thumbs, tiny little creatures who have to be carried carefully; or there are children whose faces suddenly transform, so that a joyful child's face suddenly becomes a wise old face. These children also appear in the oddest places in dreams. A little bundle with a child in it is suddenly found lying on a windowsill, or a child is simply there, not having exactly been born, but making its presence known by loud crying and demands far beyond its age.

Children that we dream of at this time of life often do not stand for actual children, even though many women are still bearing children in midlife; they are special, meaningful children who best symbolize the new psychological orientation. Once again a future exists! An orientation toward death does not come to us right away in the form of an attitude of sitting around doing nothing but resignedly waiting for the end. Orienting oneself toward life's end, as I have noted, means essentialization, a further step in self-development. The dream children of midlife evoke the same feelings that one feels when actual children are born: joy, happiness, bliss, and an intense orientation toward the future. A small child requires of his parents total involvement in his minutest changes, adaptability, a willingness to adapt to his growth needs. And these are precisely the feelings that are also necessary in midlife, when typically one has settled into the comfort of the daily routine and boredom arises all too often. The dream child reveals to the dreamer (at first only in dream life) forgotten feelings of awakening that bring new zest. These are the very feelings that are essential to getting through the transition from life's noon to its evening. The child in the dreams, even though we may not know what it means, is new life proclaiming itself, asking to be honored, cherished, and cared for by us as our highest value. The dream child asks of us different attitudes, ones that contradict our former routine attitudes. No doubt this involves an orientation toward the end of life; however, this orientation—and therein lies the contradiction—is at the same time new life. I consider it profoundly meaningful that dreams at midlife often involve children. It is not ourselves that we are rejuvenating but rather something outside of ourselves. This new life proclaiming itself demands that we take responsibility. We are responsible for the second half of our lives. It is a task that we cannot evade, just as most of us could not evade the responsibilities of actual parenthood.

The Grimm's fairy tale "Rumpelstiltskin" describes such a life transition through its images, among which the symbol of the child plays a key role. In this familiar tale, a father hands over his daughter to a suitor with a lie: his daughter, he boasts, can spin straw into gold! What suitor would turn down a deal like that! And so the father is free of his daughter, and the king's son has a captive who will make him rich. For the fairy tale heroine alone the situation is difficult and even agonizing—how is she supposed to make gold out of straw? Let us pause for a moment and try to translate the imagery of the fairy tale into practical terms so that we can understand it.

There are definitely fathers who praise their daughters beyond their worth, never accepting their true nature, but seeing them as far better than they are. Usually it happens this way: the father boasts about his daughter, telling whoever will listen how clever and charming she is. But at home, where no one else can hear or see, he changes his tune. Then there is the report card brought home from school, dismissed with the remark, "Next time it must be better!" Or the father may catch his daughter standing in front of the mirror and casually drop a disparaging remark about her appearance, implying that she will never catch a man. Even worse is the example of the father who tells the girl's mother that it is high time she got a bra. Tossed in this way between praise and disparagement, the daughter is left with a feeling of inadequacy. In the future she will bend over backward to win back the loving, proud daddy of her early childhood, to become his sunshine once more.

Even when a daughter has not lived at home for years, having cut the umbilical cord with her parents, she carries the feeling of inadequacy with her and constantly strives to achieve a sense of adequacy. She may begin to live beyond her means, create untenable situations, take on more work than she can handle, pretend to know more than she does and be able to do more than she can. She wears clothes she cannot afford and feigns more pleasure in intimate relations with her partner than she actually experiences. Her father lives on in her as an inner authority that drives her to succeed. Without success she would feel as miserable as she once did at home, where derogatory remarks about her were the order of the day. If she marries, she feels compelled to maintain this high level at any cost. She must be perfect and bring family, career, and everything associated with them up to par. She often does this at the cost of her health, needing tranquilizers to achieve the serene and sweet femininity for which she is beloved. Of course, she is also bright and clever.

Such a situation cannot continue, for the inner emptiness begins to come through; her inner resources are progressively drained. She may reach the point where she can no longer keep the whole show going. She begins to notice that she has lived for an ideal of perfection and has sacrificed everything to it, above all her own development. A person who has to turn straw into gold lives under stress. She may appear to have a perfect marriage and the best-brought-up children and may be valued for her professional ability and in demand for honorary social duties in the community. Meanwhile she has repeated in her life what her father did to her: he bragged about her to friends and relatives and used her to satisfy his own needs for recognition and response.

Let us return to the fairy tale. Who helps the heroine to spin straw into gold? It is a gnome, Rumpelstiltskin. In developing consciousness about a lifestyle like the one I have just described, it is essential—and means a step toward further maturation—for the ego to differentiate itself from its psychological background, to become aware of itself as distinct from Rumpelstiltskin. In relation to our example, this means understanding that the ego and the father complex are two different things. As Jung showed, such autonomous complexes function as fragmentary personalities and behave as such in the inner world of the psyche. It is extremely important for the ego to disengage itself from identification with them. This usually takes a long time, because the unconscious foundations of our character and actions are not recognizable from the outset. We just behave in thus-and-such a way in an unquestioning and unreflecting manner.

The woman in our example did not see that her father complex was causing her to live a life that proceeded at the cost of her own inner development. She could not see that a Rumpelstiltskin was constantly at work in her, leading her on to still more perfect action. And for what purpose? To please, to fulfill the image that her father had made of her and that had been replicated in her relationship with her husband. She had become a woman who fulfilled the expectations of men. She satisfied the anima of her husband just as she had the anima of her father. In other words, the unconscious image of the feminine in her father and husband had a compelling quality for her, demanding that she live up to it. The fact that she did so also had to do with her mother, who had set an example for her of a life in which a woman has to fulfill a man's expectations. In so doing she had done her daughter a disservice and created a faulty basis for the girl's independent development. As in reality, the mother in the fairy tale did not intervene, did not stand in the way of the "sale" of her daughter.

Only analysis can help in a case like this. In many such cases, the impulse toward change and transformation arises in midlife, at the point when the inherited life pattern has been sufficiently fulfilled and the yearning for one's own autonomous development begins to make its presence felt in the depths of the soul. In analysis the first order of business is to become aware of one's childhood and to learn to see the ways in which an unconscious father complex can shape one's life.

How long will the cruel game continue? How long must the fairy-tale heroine keep enlisting Rumpelstiltskin's help to make gold from straw? When Rumpelstiltskin is called upon to save her for the third time, he demands the heroine's child. The only way she can save her child is to discover his name.

The woman we have been describing reached a crisis in midlife in which she experienced great disorientation. In a lengthy analysis she reflected on her approach to life, and in the process learned to differentiate the father complex—the inner Rumpelstiltskin—from herself. She succeeded gradually in freeing herself from the paternal pressure that had shaped her life up to this point. By doing this she became more open to aspects of life that had hitherto been given short shrift: leisure, feeling-based values, hobbies, and refinement of her talents. She began to set aside part of her days for activities that were purposeless, playful, without stress or pressure to succeed or produce. A dream that impressed her at this time was the following:

> There is a golden hamster near me that changes into a child. I love this child dearly and feel deeply connected to her. The child is a retarded child, whom I have to teach a lot. I find myself with her in a garden where there is a playground setup that I built before last winter. There are little shrubs and houses; a little stream winds through it; flowers, crocuses and others, are coming up in between. I play with the child here. The child successfully pushes a wool thread under a little piece of material. This simple action requires great concentration and dexterity from the child. I am immensely happy that she succeeds in pushing the thread under the material. It is a completely different pleasure than I have ever known before. It is pleasure over the child's success at something difficult. I feel her pride and pleasure.

The dream was immediately clear to her; it told her what she had to do now was get free of the golden hamster. The hamster she understood to be her former activity and goals, which had been oriented too one-sidedly toward security and earning money. How precisely the dreams had chosen the symbol: a golden hamster hoards for security, and its color refers to gold, or money. She understood that behind it was concealed a retarded child, a child left behind, to whom she now wanted to devote herself. She drew courage from the dream. It showed her as someone who was definitely able to devote herself to the child. She gets involved in the small-scale playground scene, identifying with the child's sense of size and scale, and plays with her, teaching her simple skills at the same time. The joy that she feels over the child's success is a deep, motherly one; it is not pleasure in her own achievement but rather satisfaction at the child's progress. The child seems to stand for all those sides of her personality that previously had to be left behind in her life but were now demanding integration. These new sides of her did not demand sacrificing her professional orientation but wanted to be on equal footing with it. The child was also a promise of a new life, of a newly bestowed future in which her nature would develop beyond the one-sided business orientation toward greater wholeness. Things hitherto not experienced became important and began to give her great satisfaction. Her attitude toward life as a whole was transformed. Life appeared to her now as something to be responsible for in the way that a mother feels responsible for her child. She did not give up her career but began to experience it differently. Work was experienced less as stress than as a task to which she could dedicate herself increasingly in loving devotion. Another striking dream of hers was this one:

> I have taken the place of my former nursery-school teacher and now work as a nursery-school teacher. Someone tells me my nursery-school teacher has retired. I have an injured child in my lap, and I attend to her lovingly. She resembles me as a child. This is an absolutely unfamiliar situation in which I do not appear to fit at all. But it is remarkably pleasing to me, and more and more things occur to me that I could do with the children. I am astonished by this. Finally, though, I decide it is a good idea to rearrange my life accordingly and work half time in my regular profession and half time as a nursery-school teacher. I will be able to manage that, too, since I do not have to be in the nursery school around the clock but rather only for specific hours. Such thoughts and others go through my mind in the dream, and again and again I am astonished that I want to do this, that I can do it, that I am able to cope with the unfamiliarity of it and even enjoy it.

This dream resembles the hamster dream insofar as it also deals with a child in need of care and attention. Again the dreamer gives these to a great extent. She has the experience of being able to do something and even take pleasure in it— something she had never experienced before. Now she will arrange her life differently and be increasingly open to the new sides of her experience.

Let us consider for a moment how what has been said up to now relates to the tale of Rumpelstiltskin. At the moment when Rumpelstiltskin demands the child, the story begins to move toward a different ending than the one we expected at the beginning. The change in our heroine's actions is this: she will not give up the child; the child is not to be sacrificed, for it is more precious than straw spun into gold. She sends her helpers and helpers' helpers out in every direction to discover the problematic unknown name. In other words, she engages her whole being, all her abilities, to save the child. The midlife crisis demands such a commitment; it challenges us totally. But despite our being totally challenged, ultimately whether things turn out well or not does not depend on us but on chance. The matter is portrayed this way in the fairy tale, too: the name is learned by accident. Psychological change and new orientation are paradoxical; they challenge all our capacities, and yet the transformation is dependent not on us but on chance. Jung described this with the expression *Deo concedente*: God willing, the transformation is a success. The gnome is discovered and his name is overheard as he absentmindedly sings the well-known lines:

> Roast today, tomorrow bake,
> After that the child I'll take,
> And sad the queen will be to lose it,
> Rumpelstiltskin is my name;
> Luckily no one knows it.

Rumpelstiltskin is recognized, and the child is allowed to live. In my opinion a perfection-oriented woman, who on top of this also experiences a conflict between family and career, only discovers her true character when she recognizes and names the father complex that has driven her to unrelenting labor her whole life long. Naming something means knowing it and having power over it. Discovery occurs in the fairy tale through finding Rumpelstiltskin in a distant place. We find insight psychologically by tracking down the complex in our psychic landscape and learning about it. What happens in the fairy tale once and for all must occur in life not once but countless times. The complex must be experienced, suffered through, and recognized again and again for us to be able to break its spell.

The Gospel of Saint Matthew (12:43–45) gives an account of the casting out of an evil spirit with God's help. The demon or evil spirit talks to himself and asks himself where he should direct his steps. Then it occurs to him that he could turn around and go back, and shortly thereafter he arrives at his former abode, which is now beautifully ordered and decorated. Then he returns and brings seven other evil spirits right along with him. The psychological meaning of this story is that a harmful complex can indeed be recognized and driven out, but to overcome it completely, further vigilance is needed. Instead of exercising further vigilance, it seems the man in the Gospel story rested too naively in a sense of well-being.

Viewed as a whole, the fairy tale represents a major change in a woman's relationship to her work. In my opinion, a woman can do the work required of her without stress, pain, and conflict only when she accepts herself as she would a child for whom she feels responsible, recognizing her talent and taking the attitude reflected in the saying, "A gift is a responsibility." Only then is she free and able to accomplish her activities in a way that fully expresses feminine relatedness. The unfortunate conflict between two areas of responsibility, family and career, is resolved in the symbol of the child. Thus the symbolic child of midlife challenges us to integrate hitherto unexplored aspects of ourselves and to strive for wholeness.

THE REALM OF DEATH

Death is the last new beginning that we humans undertake. This is a beginning of a quite different kind than the transitions we have previously gone through. If the individual experiences himself as alone in life, this solitude is only apparent; similar situations are experienced by other people too, and if one is only willing, one can establish a relationship with others' life experiences through discussion and reading, and in that way reduce the feeling of loneliness. In death, by contrast, we are truly alone; we must endure it alone, and no one knows what comes afterward.

Interestingly, the symbol of the child is also found in the realm of death. Fantasies and dreams of dying people sometimes revolve around childhood and the symbol of the child. The appearance of the child in this last segment of life appears to represent a new stage of change. The idea of death as a new birth is age-old. In antiquity, many peoples buried their dead curled up in the fetal position. Sometimes they used a correspondingly shaped container as a coffin. This form of burial expresses the idea that human beings, born as children, in death return to the primordial ground of creation as children once again.

From ancient tradition also stems the notion of the telluric origin of the child. Children come from the water, from the earth. Thus it was and to some extent still is the custom today to lay a newborn child on the ground and have its father raise it up, betokening its origin in the earth, the transpersonal mother. We still have a reflection of this widespread idea in the popular belief that children come from the "child pond." The belief in the stork also is an expression of this idea. The stork fetches the child from the marshes and delivers it to its future parents. From the earth we come and to earth we return. The Bible expresses this idea in the following words: "For dust you are and to dust you shall return" (Eccles. 3:20). Throughout the world there are death and burial rites based on the belief that in death the human being again becomes a child of Mother Earth and thus reenters the cycle of constantly renewed life.

If the child, birth, and the beginning of life constitute a unity, which of course cannot be conceptualized, it seems to me that there is also a certain connection between death and the child. This idea is not based only on the beliefs and rituals that I have just mentioned; it also arises in the dreams and fantasies of the dying. The idea of such a connection occurred to me, however, when I noticed that in Latin the term for grandson, originally *avunculus*, means "little grandfather." This is linked with the idea that the grandfather, or rather his soul, is incarnated as an ancestral soul in the grandchild. Thus the souls of dying members of the family are mysteriously connected to the children being born.

This idea appeared in the following dream of a forty-year-old woman who was in a crisis that was to renew her life. In the dream an old man dies. The dreamer looks into the casket and, to her great astonishment, discovers in it a small child. The dream refers clearly in its symbolic images to the cyclical renewal of life:

> I went to a burial. A famous old man, a patriarch, had died. The entire large family went to the burial. Parents of schoolchildren were there too. We were waiting for the minister. On pine boards around the casket stood little figures, probably made by the grandchildren. I found this odd as a gift for a deceased person.
>
> The minister came. We could have one more look at the dead person. I glanced into the casket; but there was a very small child in it. And it was still alive. I was startled and thought: This is completely wrong! It is still alive! Doubt. Should I stop the funeral service? He must be given another chance. One just doesn't bury a live child.

To be sure, actual death was not the issue for this woman, but her inner transformation was expressing itself as a death and rebirth, symbolized by the old man and his transformation into a child. The grandfather-grandchild connection is symbolized in the dream by the grandchildren's gifts arranged around the casket.

Finally, the fantasies of a woman dying of cancer, which also suggested the idea of a cyclical renewal of life even in death, made a big impression on me. Twice I was present as this woman came to her senses out of a delirious state and very clearly and insistently congratulated her daughter on the birth of a girl. This was not an expression of delirium but seemed to me to be an allusion to the mysterious ancestor, a message that life does not end in death but rather renews itself. Through her death, as I saw it, a spiritual potential was freed, which she attributed to the fantasy child of her daughter. Life stood in a mysterious connection to death, and death was not an ending but rather a new beginning.

Let us conclude this section with a vivid dream that another woman with cancer dreamed a week before her death. In a remarkable and consoling manner, death is portrayed as a merging into the Great Mother. Death from this point of view is an empowerment to become a child again in the womb of a greater power.

> I slip under the coat of a divine female figure. My father is already there, but there are other people under this coat too. The coat is black, the female figure larger than life. Under her coat I feel safe.

When the woman had dreamed this dream, she was certain that she would be dying soon, although the doctors were not expecting her death for a while. She told the dream to a woman preacher who visited her regularly and asked her to tell the dream to a lot of people to let them know that there is something comforting even in death. As a result of the dream the sick woman's fears abated, and she faced her end calmly and courageously. The large woman under whose coat she had been able to slip in the dream strongly recalls the Madonna, who, with her protective cloak, offers many people protection—an image that has inspired numerous artists. In the divine woman the mother goddess appears as a sheltering figure to whom the individual returns as a child at death.

3   The Divine and Holy Child

THE FOLLOWING DREAM of the writer Friedrich Huch (1873–
1913), a nephew of the poet Ricarda Huch, has been preserved:

> I go into an old house alone. Inside is a single, high-
> ceilinged, enormous room like in a church. In the middle are
> altar steps; at the top sits a child. I go over to him, throw
> myself down before him, embrace him, and break into sobs.[1]

The context in which Huch dreamed this dream is not known; nor
can we say anything about the life situation that the dream was
related to, or how the dream may have influenced it. The dream
impresses us with its simplicity and its deep, shattering emotion,
which breaks through in the sobs. We encounter a tremendous
tension: suspecting nothing, the dreamer goes into an old house
the interior of which proves to be a church. In the middle of it,
elevated on steps, sits a child. Captivated by this figure, the
dreamer is shaken to the core, falls down on his knees, and embraces the child in a gesture of humility and devotion. It becomes
immediately clear that this is a special, holy child, who, when
elevated as a central figure, can affect people profoundly.[2]

THE CHRIST CHILD

In the Christian religion the model for a holy child like the
one in the dream is Jesus, who was born as a divine child in the
darkness of night and in great poverty, as the stories of his birth
in the gospels of Matthew and Luke tell us. The child is simul-
taneously divine and holy. The adjectives *divine* and *holy* refer
on the one hand to his divine origin and, on the other, to his
effect on the human soul. That which is divine has a holy effect,
inspires holy feelings in us, and has something about it that is
wholesome and healing, that makes us whole.

Jesus in his appearance as divine child is the focal point of

Christmas year after year. His miraculous birth, the adoration by the shepherds and the three kings, who with their oxen and donkeys gathered around the manger in the stable in Bethlehem, has drawn the attention of artists as no other event in history has. Depictions of it are innumerable, and it is a scene that has deeply stirred many hearts.

The birth heralded by the star of Bethlehem had been foretold to Joseph long before by an angel of the Lord in a dream: "Joseph son of David, do not be afraid to take Mary home as your wife, because she has conceived what is in her by the Holy Spirit" (Matt. 1:20).

Not long afterward Joseph had another dream. It referred to the danger Jesus faces from Herod and to the planned Massacre of the Innocents: ". . . the angel of the Lord appeared to Joseph in a dream and said, 'Get up, take the child and his mother with you, and escape into Egypt, and stay there until I tell you, because Herod intends to search for the child and do away with him' " (Matt. 2:13).

A third time the angel appeared in a dream to Joseph. He was told to return home from Egypt, thus preparing the future mission of Jesus to Israel: "Get up, take the child and his mother with you and go back to the land of Israel, for those who wanted to kill the child are dead" (Matt. 2:19–20).

Joseph heeded his dreams and did as the angel of the Lord told him. We might deduce from this that in their deepest levels our dreams manifest a mysterious connection with the source of all things and that from time to time we receive hints from them pointing out our way, if we are only willing to take them seriously. Ultimately, it is the soul of the individual person that has the ability to respond to difficulty and distress. On the whole, a great deal depends on the individual. This kind of perspective on individual responsibility and worth tends to fall more and more by the wayside as we put ever more emphasis on calling loudly for social and political change. It is not so much outside in the world but within us that new beginnings and potential transformations begin to show themselves.

The Christmas story tells about the birth of the divine in the human soul. The child is begotten not by a human being but by the Holy Spirit. This is an expression of the fact that here we have to do with something that is wholly other, that belongs to another dimension beyond the human. Something is taking place within the psyche that requires our special and entire attention.

The divine child was borne by Mary. Who is Mary in us and which qualities are symbolized by her? Mary is the embodiment and model of the feminine in each of us, regardless of whether we are male or female. That which is new is prepared in our feelings, not in our intellect. Mary also stands for the unconscious and our dream world; in these realms the future begins to germinate and from there communicate itself to our daytime consciousness, which Joseph represents. Mary and Joseph can be viewed as the two distinct modes of human consciousness. There are various designations for these, such as patriarchal and matriarchal consciousness or masculine and feminine consciousness. I prefer to speak of day and night consciousness. In night consciousness we are in touch with the unconscious, with dreams, feelings, and the flow of time. In day consciousness we strive for objectivity, clarity, stability, and sense of purpose. Together the two modes form a whole and in optimal circumstances they affect each other in such a way that something new, symbolized by the child, can arise.

It is Mary who carries the Christ child in her arms, and it is this same Mary who holds her dead son on her lap in pietà depictions such as the one by Michelangelo in Saint Peter's in Rome. The two most important moments in the life of Jesus, the beginning and end of human existence—birth and death—are linked to the symbol of the mother. We might well ponder our whole life long on the meaning of this—a fresh look at it is always in order. To protect, nurture, and care for a young life requires feminine attitudes; to accept and bear death once again requires the mother and her feminine qualities. Mary holds a divine figure, Jesus, at the beginning and end of his life. Mary as the simple maiden, as the Evangelist calls her, represents each of us, offering us a model of behavior, a way of relating to the divine, calling on us to follow her in opening ourselves to the religious experience.

What further meanings lie in the symbol of Mary with her child, her son? The divine in each of us is as tender and in need of protection as a small child. But what is this "divine in us?" It is, I think, many things that can be only inadequately and incompletely described. One is our likeness to the image of God, the divine spark in each person, which can be felt in those moments when we are able to have the intuitive sense that we are doing the right thing and going the right way. Furthermore, the divine in us is our striving to become what we are and to allow our own natural abilities to be realized. It is also our ability to believe that, despite all distress and suffering, there is a God who grants us the "courage to be," in Paul Tillich's phrase. And last, we could call divine those experiences in which we are able to experience grace. Feminine attitudes are appropriate with respect to these moments, attitudes of patience in suffering, of openness, of endurance. Strong masculine faith is ultimately footed in feminine, feeling-level receptivity.

We can see from the behavior of a mother toward her child that the child needs the unconditionality of religious devotion as well as constancy, love, and nourishment in a figurative sense. Also important is an acceptance of that which is developing. Mary had to accept Jesus' turning away from his parents and following One who was greater than he (Luke 2:41–52). With a physical child, parents must take a positive attitude toward what develops in the child. For that reason an attitude of acceptance is important, because the life unfolding in a child is often not what we wish for, demand, and want for that child. The same is true for our life experiences altogether. What happens to us and is fulfilled as our destiny is a part of our life and demands acceptance, assimilation, and devotion, even if it is a great blow of fate like that prefigured and symbolized by Mary and her dead son. For such an occurrence to become a blessing for us, it appears to me necessary to accept the grief and shock into ourselves, to mourn the misfortune and allow it a place in our feelings—endure it. We must also be willing to heed the messages of dreams.[3]

In this connection I am reminded of a woman whose only son died suddenly in an accident when he was still a child. For days before the tragic event she had the following dream, which at that time she could not make sense of:

> I am standing with many, many people on the street in pouring rain. Gradually a procession forms from the many people and moves toward a grotto. People are saying that someone is going to be blessed. Who might that be? I wonder. Then: Certainly not I. It is raining without letup. Then we are near the grotto. Suddenly I am in the grotto and am being blessed by a large feminine figure. She reminds me of Mary. I am seized by a feeling I never experienced before.

Although the dream moved her deeply, she only remembered it several days after her son's accidental death in the midst of her grief. It seemed connected to the event, but just how was not clear to her at the time. The dream stayed with her through the years and decades; it was enigmatic yet sometimes also comforting. Her son's death never struck her as a blessing, yet years later she could say in retrospect that this dream had taught her a great deal. It taught her to accept loss and consciously bear it. It was her way of working with this blow of fate that turned it into a blessing. Until then she had been, she thought, more oriented toward the masculine approach, fascinated by the possibility of unlimited accomplishment. The loss of her son led her gradually to a new orientation and a different relationship to life in general. In those dark hours, Mary had become a model for her, for Mary also had had to suffer the death of her son. The blessing of all this turned out to be that this woman learned to accept life as a mystery, something that could not be predicted or planned out in advance. Here, too, the religious question, hitherto unexamined, found its place. In this sense the woman had made the divine—which she had encountered in this blow of fate as something terrible—human. From this awful experience, which always remained awful for her, she was able to draw a blessing.

Let us return to the Christmas story. The divine child brings something new and has kings and shepherds, oxen and donkeys, as well as his parents, Mary and Joseph, bowing down to him and worshiping him. The simple, everyday element, our shepherd side, and our value systems, represented by the three kings, must devote themselves to the child and the new experience. The woman whose child died in an accident allowed this experience into her everyday life and permitted her regally elevated values gradually to give way to other, wiser ones.

Why are the ox and the donkey always included in the Christmas story when nowhere in the New Testament is there a mention of them? There are scholarly interpretations for this; theologists turn for an explanation to Isaiah 1:3: "The ox knows its owner and the ass its master's manger." Also, in following the church fathers, the ox has been regarded as the representative of Judaism and the donkey of paganism. Beyond these explanations we may also offer a psychological interpretation. The holy family in the stable in Bethlehem with the shepherds and the kings does not alone constitute the proper surroundings of Christ's birth. In truth the sacred depictions symbolize our own psychological world, in whose innermost part is the manger, which is the vessel and place where the "word" can become flesh, where the divine finds a dwelling place in the human being. There, where the miracle of God becoming human occurs, the entirety of our humanness is called upon. Thus it is not by chance that the animals, the ox and donkey, as representatives of our instinctual side, are assembled around this spiritual focal point. In addition to our everyday lives, symbolized by the shepherds, and our value systems, symbolized by the kings, the animals need to be present too. Just as our corporeality is present as a witness to the divine birth, so the ox and donkey are essential too. Faith always means total faith—with body and soul.

Yet the child has hardly been born before he is threatened by Herod. Scarcely do forces stir in us for our healing than counterforces are awakened which, like Herod, will not tolerate anything new near them or elevated above them. Everything has to stay the same old way, because change is always hard work and, from time to time, painful.

The Threat to the Holy Child

What does the holy child stand for in us? I think it represents our own potential and talents, which are to be developed ac-

cording to God's urging. The divine child is always a holy child
too. In addition to the wealth of meaning it has in the religious
context, the word *holy* always also has a sense of wholesome-
ness, health, and wholeness. The divine child is therefore one
that can awaken feelings in us redolent of health and wholeness.

How much we, like Herod, fight against the holy child in us
is shown in the parable of the talents (Matt. 25:14–30). In this
parable, the head of the household travels out of the country,
entrusting his worldly possessions to his servants. To the first he
gives five talents, to the second two, and to the third one talent
to hold in trust. Upon his return he praises the first two servants
because they have increased his property; but the third, who
buried the talent and risked nothing, he reproaches and con-
signs to "the darkness," where there will be "wailing and gnashing of teeth." Obviously the first two servants acted correctly and
increased the property. Here the term *talent* should not be understood to mean not only material possessions but also a gift, or
talent. The meaning of this parable is that we should make the
most of our abilities and not hide our light under a bushel. What
of the third servant, who buried his talent? Is he also perhaps to
be understood as a part of us? Are we not all too often inclined
to bury, conceal, and deny our gifts? I am not thinking primarily
of obvious talents that our parents and teachers have encouraged; I am thinking of those moments in which we persist in
comparing ourselves with others and their talents. When we do
this, our own potential is disempowered, alienated from us;
finally, there is little more we can do with it. In these moments
the little humpbacked man is at work, spoiling everything for us.
In a well-known song from *Des Knaben Wunderhorn* (The Youth's
Cornucopia), a nineteenth-century collection of German folk
songs, we find: "When I in my kitchen go / To set my soup
a-cookin', / There's that little humpbacked man, / He has my
pot a-broken." In such moments we get in our own way and
sabotage ourselves.

There are other counterforces that help us bury our talent aside
from the tiresome business of self-comparison. There are also
caretakers who want children to be different from the way they

really are and ignore their actual potential. Initially, we only get away from such figures on the outer level. Within us, they continue to have an effect. Long since a part of our own ego, they go on telling us we should be different or—even worse—that we are worthless.

Other counterforces are obstructive conventions. Some in particular plague women who want to realize their talents. The idea that women belong in the bosom of the family, along with many other ideas like it, is familiar to most readers. These counterforces must be recognized and brought to consciousness. We need to put a stop to them, but at the same time we must realize that fundamentally we are the ones who are burying our own talent.

In this connection I think of a younger man who came into analysis because he could never get anywhere in his career. In his past were unfavorable circumstances, troublesome illnesses, and broken-off studies. He had had to live in places where continuing his education was difficult and had had to move from one linguistic area of Switzerland to another. He believed these circumstances sufficiently explained why he could not improve his fortunes. But then he had a vivid dream, which caused him to view the matter from another angle.

> I am standing in a room and looking out the window. I see a woman and know too that I have seen her many times before. She is carrying a child in her arms. She buries this child day after day.

As it turned out, he had such a woman within him as well. A side of him daily buried hope, zest, and enterprise under a mountain of abortive and pessimistic thoughts. To return to the biblical parable, he was like the third servant who never succeeded in making the talent he was given bear interest. In him lived the deeply embedded conviction that he had no right to his own life. The child symbolized his own life, which was not allowed to exist, was blocked in its development again and again. This dream made him dramatically aware that outer circumstances represented only one side of the truth. The other lay in himself and his self-sabotage. In the course of time, as a result of his self-burial, he fell into the darkness, the wailing, and the gnashing of teeth. He no longer saw any way out and got himself more and more entangled in a web of negative thoughts, defiant rebellion, and moral cowardice. It required long and patient therapeutic-analytical work to come to recognize the hindering forces and causes, so as to make room for a stable feeling of self-esteem. The child buried daily in the dream was his inner self. To the extent that we are inclined to understand our nature and natural tendencies in a religious framework, when we behave like the third servant in the parable, our connection to the transcendent, our *re-ligio* (re-connection) is put into question. Therefore, in therapy or outside of it, it is important always to do justice to the self and be aware of our reconnection to it.

The Divine Child and the Religious Dimension

A fifty-year-old woman, whom I shall call Sabine, had the following two dreams, one right after the other:

> I am in an airplane flying south. It is time to get off the plane, and I go to the back to get my luggage. I see to my great astonishment that a new piece of luggage has been added. It is an open, blue canvas suitcase that is covered with pink silk on the inside. In it is a tiny child, not much larger than a hand. Tremendous serenity comes over me as I look at this child, and carefully I take the suitcase with the child in my arms. I can no longer carry my heavy suitcases, though. My two sons, who are also there, will take care of these pieces of luggage. Happily I walk toward the front with the child, looking at her again and again. At the same time the fear that I could hurt the child, do something to her, seizes me.

> I am in my house and have a clock beside me that I have to hang. But I am not sure where it should go. Suddenly I have a second clock. I decide to hang the first clock, a pendulum clock with a black case, in the living room. The other clock has changed in the meantime. Now it looks like an open window at whose sides white sheer curtains are hanging. At the top is mounted an icon that represents the Madonna and Child. I hang this clock near my desk.

Both dreams show surprise. In the first, the dreamer unex
pectedly encounters the tiny child and experiences a bliss never
known before. In the second dream, suddenly in addition to her
old familiar clock, she has another one, which is quite special.
This is also a surprise and in this case, too, she has a new
experience. The dreams indicate changes of a kind that were
still unknown at the time of the dreams. Sabine was, however,
quite moved by the dream events. In her memory, she again and
again savored the feelings that had arisen in the dreams, and
loved to linger over both of them in her thoughts. She found
them quite extraordinary and special.

She experienced as extraordinary the strong reference to the
mother-child relationship. In the first dream she experienced
herself as maternal toward the child in a way she had never
known. In the second dream the marvelous image of the mother
and child on the icon appeared.

Only later was it possible to understand the dreams completely, however. For these dreams, it was quite particularly the
case that they contained prefigurations of the future. For this
reason, we must now recount something of Sabine's life story,
her experience of herself and the world, as well as something of
the period following the dreams.

The fear expressed in the first dream that she might somehow
hurt the child may serve as our point of departure. Sabine had
come to therapy because she was plagued by this and other similar destructive thoughts. Thoughts that come to mind despite our
conscious intent are called overdetermined ideas. When they are
stronger still and arise compulsively, they are called compulsive
thoughts. Sabine was horrified about these thoughts, which completely demoralized and frightened her. In addition, understandably she had not told anyone about them, and even could not do
so. This led to strong feelings of isolation, in which the thoughts
finally became a morbid secret that was a great burden to her.

Sabine had previously made several brief attempts at therapy
with me and had also had psychiatric treatment for a short time.
The diagnosis was compulsion neurosis or anxiety neurosis with
compulsive elements. In addition to verbal therapy she was

treated with tranquilizers, which gave her temporary relief. Since Sabine was in treatment with her various therapists only briefly each time, I suspect that the depression linked to the symptom of compulsive thoughts had not been noticed, and probably also Sabine herself could not admit to depression. In this way the unexplained, crippling symptom remained in the foreground and blocked the view of the whole picture. It may be noted at this point that, unfortunately, it frequently occurs in therapeutic practice that the depressive syndrome is ignored because foreground symptoms such as anxiety and the over-determined ideas of anxiety neurosis or compulsion neurosis become the primary theme. In actual fact Sabine had overvaluated abusive ideas or thoughts of doing harm, which is a frequent occurrence in connection with depression. Sabine's condition could be traced back a good twenty years in her life, during which they appeared after longer and shorter intervals.

The fear in the first dream was thus real for the dreamer, being related with this illness, which she was aware of. But the dream also showed her deep beatific feeling for the child. She, who was understandably afraid of children and where possible even avoided them because of her thoughts of harming them, experienced herself in the dream behaving maternally toward a child for the first time. Sabine's inner difficulties were hardly noticeable on the outside. She was always capable of bearing this burden and fulfilled the tasks that lay before her.

Research into Sabine's childhood brought to light that she had started her life in difficult circumstances. Her mother suffered from tuberculosis and was often away for months at a time because of sanatorium stays. During this time Sabine was left with various nannies. Her mother was also never able to hold the child in her arms because of the danger of infection. Her father, an extremely active and quite busy man, loved his daughter but could not find much time for her. On the basis of this briefly outlined childhood history it became understandable that Sabine had been able to develop little confidence in herself and the world and thus lacked inner security. A negative mother complex was constellated; it caused Sabine to see herself primarily in negative terms and to think that people close to her viewed her as exclusively worthless and inferior.

Through a long period of therapy Sabine learned to separate herself from this negative view of herself. She began to understand her childhood history and finally, through confrontation with her dreams, to be aware of her unconscious and benefit from its positive influences.

The critical times in which the compulsive thoughts appeared again continued, though with lesser intensity. Sabine could meanwhile clearly recognize the depressions linked with these thoughts, and it became possible for her to recognize the painful events as an actual illness and, when necessary, to make use of medication.[4]

Between the depressive, dark periods, Sabine now enjoyed the good times more and radiated cheerfulness. At the time of the dream described above, she was in a good phase, in full possession of her energy, and she kept even the thought of the repetition of a dark phase far away from her mind. The dreams had made her happy and open, willing to take on new challenges. She was full of plans and enthusiasm for work. By profession a scientific journalist, she had used her writing talent now and then through the years to write down her own thoughts in poetry and prose. But this talent never came to full fruition because Sabine could never believe in herself enough, owing to her lack of confidence. As a result, each time, she put what she had written away in a drawer and forgot about it. It was easier for her to put her energy into work assigned to her by the newspaper than to create something herself. Indeed it is not impossible that her depression was also linked to insufficient cultivation of this talent.

A short time after the dreams the familiar depressive, psychological immobilization befell Sabine, and it was not long before the brooding and offensive thoughts appeared. In the course of this affliction, which lasted for months, there were moments when she had to give up on all the aids she had relied on in the past. To the depression were added severe anxiety attacks, and she had to simply surrender herself, give herself over to what was happening to her. Then one day she found the old family Bible; it had

lain forgotten for years after her mother's death in a chest of draw-
ers. In reading it she discovered many passages that had been
underlined by her grandmother, whom she had loved dearly. An
invisible bond began to grow up between her and this kindly,
sustaining maternal figure, which also strengthened the maternal
potential in herself. The dream experience in which she saw herself as a mother relating to a small child seemed to have become
a reality. Having come to the end of her resources, she now miraculously found solace in these old texts as she chanced upon
uplifting passages that helped her endure the darkness. The
Psalms appealed to her most of all. She found in them an expression of mankind's lament and encountered verses that artic-
ulated her own suffering. She valued two passages most. One
expressed the full intensity of depression in its existential actuality: "Death's cords were tightening around me, the nooses of
Hell; distress and anguish gripped me" (Ps. 116:3). She understood the lament in these lines and also realized that times of
darkness, not only the good, happy times, are sent by God. She
experienced her deep distress as connected with a sense of God's
being hidden and spoke of a period of time in which God was
absent from her and she was without any sure ground. In church
she had heard only of a radiant, kindly God; now she accepted
with relief that such dark periods are also a part of God's will.

The other passage that impressed her was a comforting one. It
reads: "You need not fear the terrors of night, the arrow that flies
in the daytime; the plague that stalks in the dark" (Ps. 91:5–6).

Sabine had never really received religious education, but
during this time she had moments of belief and became conscious of what faith is. Faith is really faith when it comes out of
the darkness; only then does its redemptive quality become
evident. On this point, she wrote the following lines: "In this
darkness, this fear, and this absolute despair I can do nothing
else but hold on to the knowledge that God loves me in spite of
everything. To fail to do this would be to succumb to temptation.
I am beginning to understand what faith is: it is faith that
emerges from angst and nonexistence."

Now she sometimes felt supported by this newly discovered

faith even though it was still weak. She could not avoid seeing the seed of this faith in the tiny child she had taken in her arms in the first dream described. As things began to go better for her, she observed that her writing—even though it was difficult for her—helped her survive and calmed her. Little by little she made it her task to work on it daily; she did this because of a feeling of owing it to an inner impulse of hers and also out of the newly won conviction that God did not want to destroy her. In this conviction the lines of verse from Psalm 31 had become her guide: "Let me never be ashamed."

The two dreams turned out in retrospect to be important and meaningful. That which she had feared at the end of the first dream—harming the child—proved to be significant during the long months of darkness. The child was threatened in those months; in other words her confidence and faith were in danger of being devoured, and the child as the life impulse itself was also endangered. Little by little she had to summon up strength and rely on a source outside herself in order to maintain her relationship with the little child, the symbol of germinating religious orientation.

At this time Sabine became aware of a new dimension of existence, a theme that had already been intimated in the dream about the clocks. She hung the black clock, a symbol for chronological time, in her living room. This was linked to her daily functioning during the "black" period. The other clock, which appeared in the dream as an open window crowned by an icon, symbolized another orientation toward time; it represented a window on infinity. She hung this clock near her desk. The icon of the Mother and Child reflected her profound experience that one can survive inner conflict through the qualities of motherhood depicted in it. This religious example called on her to make room in her inner life for positive thoughts and helpful possibilities. A new period began for her, one which was in God's hands. She had to secure a place for herself in this new approach.

It was meaningful to Sabine that the dream had chosen an icon, because icons are expressive in the Eastern Church (more than in Western Christianity) of the deeply rooted idea that human beings are made in the image of God. Contemplation of the icon attunes the worshiper to the divine, and provides him with a connection to it. Icons are actually windows on eternity. As images they have a compelling quality that turns the human eros toward God. During her dark period the spiritual nature of her illness dawned on Sabine. A spiritual "organ" capable of making a connection with the divine had been given to her. Such a connection is often symbolized by the divine child; this inner child is expressed especially beautifully in the icon of the *Madonna of the Sign* (figure 5).

In maintaining our focus on Sabine's experience of opening herself to the religious dimension, several other aspects of her development have been neglected. These will be given special attention now.

It was extremely important for Sabine to be able to perceive her psychic darkness as depression, that is, as an emotional illness. This perception was—as for many people afflicted with depression—especially important in enabling her not to feel completely victimized by the agonizing compulsive brooding in which the depression always appears to be one's own fault. In the process of acknowledging depression as illness, however, we should not forget the psychodynamic aspects.

From the viewpoint of analytical psychology, in depression the Great Mother archetype is constellated in her negative and devouring aspect. This was at work to such an extent in Sabine's case that not only was every life impulse shattered but also the menacing nearness to the archetypal level showed itself as abusive thoughts. The thought of being able to hurt a child was linked directly to the negative Great Mother in her life-denying and deadly aspect. Thus the abusive thoughts were more than simply shadow aspects of the personality, more than just an expression of the aggressive fantasies toward children that are encountered so often. Mothers have such fantasies at times, and it is quite important to become conscious of them, since they make up part of the shadow, which as the depth dimension of a personality unites all those elements that are repressed because they are sinister, evil, embarrassing, or underdeveloped.[5] By

FIGURE 5
Madonna of the Sign, Transylvanian icon (18th century).
Collection of Dr. S. Amberg, Kölliken.
Copyright by Buch-Kunstverlag Ettal.

contrast, Sabine's thoughts of harming were an expression of the nearness of the shadow in its archetypal dimension, the very darkness itself. People who, like Sabine, are driven so threateningly close to destruction go through the shattering experience of being threatened by absolute evil.

In retrospect several important stages of her path out of this state can be identified. It was of utmost urgency to nurture the positive-maternal forces in Sabine. Only when these became active in her psyche and the influence of a good and kind inner figure began to emerge did she attain the ability to defend herself against the darkness. Developing this ability entailed freeing herself from the overshadowing influence of the archetypal Great Mother. As a further powerful moment, she was able to relate to the divine as Mary and God as God the Father, experiencing the religious dimension previously described. Only after these steps, which took years to accomplish, did it become possible for Sabine to accept her personal shadow side and work with it. Before this point had been reached, when the shadow came up in discussion, she was always threatened by the danger of being driven destructively close to the archetypal shadow.

The person who is threatened by archetypal darkness has to first remove himself from this influence before he can withstand the encounter with the personal shadow, which includes all of our anomalous aspects. In such cases the deficiency of positive mother elements must be balanced. An increase in ego strength, urgently necessary for self-knowledge and working with one's shadow, is the fruit of overcoming this deficiency.

From the example of Sabine and her history, the enigma that frequently lies at the heart of depression becomes clearly understandable. For one thing, depression is always a psychological illness that must be recognized as such, first by the therapist but then also by the afflicted person. On the other hand, it frequently turns out that depressions, in addition to their clinical aspects, sometimes also have a spiritual side. Romano Guardini's statement is to be taken seriously: "Melancholy is something too painful, and it reaches too deeply into the roots of our human existence, for us to entrust it [only] to the psychiatrists."[6]

CREATED IN THE DIVINE IMAGE

That human beings are made like God comes to expression in the ancient idea of the *imago dei* (image of God), which is sometimes represented by the symbol of the child. The child stands for the fundamentally new and represents a "becoming-one-with-itself" of the soul in great distress and bitter conflict. In the Christian tradition the idea of God as inherent in the image of the soul goes back to Genesis 1:27: "God created man in the image of Himself, in the image of God He created him, male and female He created them."

Jung called the potential for being in contact with God the Self. This self is ultimately, among other things, the image of God in the human soul, perhaps more precisely, a reflection of God in the human soul. The Self appears in dreams and visual images from the unconscious in various forms, one of which is the divine child. In reference to this Jung wrote:

> As a special case of the motif of the "treasure hard to attain," the child motif is extremely variable and assumes every possible form, such as the precious stone, the pearl, the flower, the vessel, the golden egg, the quaternity, the gold sphere, etc. It proves to be almost interchangeable with these and similar images to an almost unlimited extent.[7]

Although it may be true that the symbol of the child is interchangeable with other symbols of the Self, it is essential to also emphasize how it differs from them. This difference can best be grasped through comparison with the symbol of the precious stone. In contrast to the child, the stone is not alive and no longer changes; it can only change the sensibility of the observer in that he keeps noticing new facets and qualities in it. One can also put a precious stone in a jewelry box without damaging it. A child will not bear such treatment; he is living and demands from us alert involvement in its most minute developmental stages. That is true not only for the actual, physical child but also for the highly elusive content of the child symbol. When my analysands ask me at any given time what the meaning of a particular symbolic child is, I simply cannot answer with certainty because, as with a real child, we do not know in which direction, and into what, the psychological content associated with it will develop. The symbolic child, however, quite certainly stands for an attitude or state of affairs that corresponds to the nature of a child. We have to relate with continual attention, care, devotion, and unconditional love to the symbolic child's still undetermined content. Attention and openness are required precisely because we do not know its exact content. This is the essential difference between the child and other, unchangeable and constant symbols for the Self, for example, the precious stone. This difference should not be forgotten. The child, being alive, challenges us in our living being; it necessitates orientation toward the future and loving involvement in all the motivations, thoughts, feelings, actions, and situations which we think are associated with the symbolic child that had been dreamed. In this sense, the child is the carrier of the Self par excellence.

It is important to note at this point that dreams often involve neglected children. They are abandoned, buried, imprisoned, packed in boxes, and so on. In interpreting such dreams, it is essential not to concentrate only on the content of the child; it may be more important to consider the necessity of appropriate care for the child. The child as a symbol of the Self in dreams is a content that is difficult to grasp, a content that demands, more than with other symbols, a responsive, loving attitude. With the two dreams of Sabine's, in which the divine child appeared as a symbol of the Self, it was not possible to say when the dreams occurred what this child meant. Certainly it stood for something new and, in the second dream, something religious. What it really was could only be seen much later. Of decisive importance was the fact that Sabine attempted to incorporate the first dream's maternal attitude into her daily life and make an effort to be open to the thoughts and feelings that she thought were connected with the symbol of the child.

The Self as it appears in the figure of the child is often that to which we give little attention. Caught up in many worldly concerns, fascinated by power and prestige, we often do not pay attention to our inner child even though in our innermost selves we know that we need to. In this connection, it seems to me to be essential to take a moment to consider the well-known Gospel passage about the child, because it is often misunderstood:

> At this time the disciples came to Jesus and said, "Who is the greatest in the kingdom of heaven?" So he called a little child to him and set the child in front of them. Then he said, "I tell you solemnly, unless you change and become like little children you will never enter the kingdom of heaven. And so, the one who makes himself as little as this child is the greatest in the kingdom of heaven. Anyone who welcomes a little child like this in my name welcomes me." (Matt. 18:1–5)

In Jesus' time children were the epitome of the lowly and inadequate and were not, as is the case today, attributed with innocence, truth, faith, hope, peace, love, and joy. Thus the call to pay heed to the child and receive him in Jesus' name often means caring for what is least valued in ourselves.

The concept of being made in the image of God becomes particularly clear and understandable when one turns to creation myths of other cultures and religions. The idea that the godhead formed human beings from clay is widespread. An example is the Egyptial god of creation, Chnum. On the potter's wheel "the god fashioned the egg, the vessel of embryonic child, and kneaded into it the seeds of life."[8] Thus he placed something of his substance into human nature.

In the Babylonian creation hymn it says: "With his flesh and his blood Nin-Hursag mixed the clay. Thus God and humans become . . . united in the clay. Another creation god, Marduk, from the same cultural area, created humanity "to allow the gods to dwell in a home which gladdened them."[10] Thus there is a connection between man and God—this is expressed especially beautifully in this phrase from the myth.

God, or the gods, need a dwelling place in humans. This concept gives meaning to human life and endows the individual with an authority involving much responsibility. The idea that

God needs human beings lends importance to the fulfillment of one's existence and attributes far-reaching significance to the individual. In this sense creation does not take place once and for all but rather can occur daily in even the most simple situation. "My" consciousness, "my" efforts for the right and the meaningful, therefore demand a "situation-ethical" orientation, one that is suited to the situation. Situation ethics demands from the individual a continually fresh consciousness, an ongoing effort. It thus requires more from us than general ethical standards and general rules. Behavior based on situation ethics has its deepest roots in the concept of the human being made in the image of god. The view that the divine needs a dwelling place in humans seems to me to be a beautiful image of this notion. Keeping this dwelling place well tended and ready is the ultimate duty of human beings. What can dwell there is, among other things, the holy, divine child.

THE DIVINE CHILD IN OTHER CULTURES

The divine child also appears outside of Christianity. This is a motif found in all places and times. Since dreams also often use the symbolism of divine children who are not Christian, it seems appropriate to attend to this theme briefly.[11]

The emergence of the god from a lotus blossom is a popular theme. For example, the Egyptian sun god, Re, emerges in the form of a child from the primordial calyx:

> This is the lotus blossom which arose at the beginning, the bouquet is green from which you emerge in the form of a child . . . the great Lotus which arose at the beginning, in the womb of its petals you were brought into the world.[12]

In another place it is said of this sun child:

> You see his light, you breathe his scent, your noses are filled with it. He is your son, emerging as a child, who brightens the land with his two eyes. . . . I bring you the lotus which came from the marsh, the eye of Re himself in his marsh, the one who is the sum total of the divine ancestors, who made

the divine ancestors, and who created everything which exists
in this land. . . . When he opens his two eyes he lights up
the two lands, he separates night from day. The gods came
from his mouth, humans from his eyes, everything came to be
through him, the child who shone in the lotus and whose
radiance gives life to all beings.[13]

In the Babylonian myth the creator god is also born as a child
who, like Re, is already omnipotent from the beginning: "Splen-
did was his figure and the expression in his eyes. Adult at his
birth, he possessed all his power from the beginning."[14]

The myth tells us that Buddha, too, came out of his mother's
womb, yet this birth was also miraculous. An abundance of
divine qualities distinguished him too:

> Calmly erect
> Not falling headlong, gloriously shining,
> Magnificently jewelled, radiant, in this way he left
> The womb, as when the sun rises.
> This overwhelming splendor was seen by all
> Who were present, but without damage to their
> Sight. To grant them the sight, he
> Moderated his light to the soft glow of the moon;
> Yet he radiated from his body in all directions
> And as the sun's light extinguishes
> The lamp's glow, so Bodhisattva's
> Godlike beauty was visible everywhere.[15]

Greek mythology is full of divine children who demonstrate as
children their fully developed divinity. Particularly notable is the
cunning messenger god Hermes, the son of the nymph Maia and
Zeus, father of the gods. Just born, he springs from his mother's
knees and is ready for any feat. As his first deed, he makes a lyre
from a turtle shell and steals the god Apollo's herd of cattle. He
is portrayed in the Homeric Hymns as extremely lively:

> Then she bore an agile, clever, winsome little boy,
> That robber and cattle thief, the guide to dreamland,
> That nocturnal scout and gatekeeper. It was to be expected
> This morning child would soon show the immortal gods
> Glorious deeds: At noon he played the lyre,
> Then evenings he stole cattle from Apollo, the archer.

> Maia bore him on the fourth day, at the beginning of the
> month.
> Since he sprang from his mother's immortal knees
> He did not remain long lying in his divine cradle.
> No!—He rose and sought out Apollo's cattle."[16]

These are only a few examples from the profusion of god figures in child form in mythology. They are too numerous to consider all of them.

Such children from the non-Christian realm also appear in the dreams of modern people. Their symbolism is altered, to be sure, but in their essential features they show an astonishing affinity with these mythological children. The following examples are illustrative. A man had the following dream.

> I find a gorgeous flower; a beguiling fragrance emanates from
> it. As I look more closely and look down into its calyx, I
> notice a tiny little child surrounded by the deep red petals of
> the flower. I know immediately that it is a special child and
> I may not pick the flower.

The dreamer understood this flower child as a reference to his feeling side, which was to become closer to him. He had never valued feelings. Frowned upon in the family he grew up in, they continued to be left out in his later life. At midlife, in response to a crisis, his feelings became more and more important to him, and he even began to orient himself in relation to them. In the dream he is not permitted to pick the flower, which meant that he should not go on suppressing the vitality of his feelings, but rather should pay more attention to them. The child in the calyx, a special one, as the dream said, had already announced the turning point in his life. It suggested the new aspect of himself which, from that point on, the dreamer sought to integrate.

A young woman dreamed about a house in which she discovered a child:

> I find myself in the house in which I lived earlier with my
> family. The house now has an addition. It seems strange to
> me, even eerie. I ask my husband to come into the annex with
> me. There I meet a happy, self-confident acquaintance who
> has just borne a child. The child is still small, hardly a few

days old, but to my astonishment he can already speak, sit up, and walk around.

This child is distinguished by his precociousness. Developmental steps of a later age are already familiar to him right after his birth. The child is reminiscent of those deities who, like Marduk and Hermes, possess all of their powers from the start. In the dream the child belongs to the happy, self-confident woman. This represents a side of the dreamer that was inadequately available to her. Rather fearful and shy by nature, she only reluctantly got involved in new things. Secretly, however, she harbored the desire to undertake a further level of education in order to be able to integrate herself into professional life again. The child, who reminded her of Hermes, showed her—in accordance with the talents and skills of this god—the plan for her further intellectual development. Later she went ahead with the training she had contemplated and thus made the addition to the house in the dream into a reality in her life. In this way she expanded her inner house, the house of her personality.[17]

THE HUMAN DIMENSION AND THE DIVINE CHILD

We project many things onto the child: innocence, spontaneity, naturalness, truth, development, harmony. We impose paradise fantasies on childhood, seeing it in terms of carefreeness, freedom, security, intimate relatedness to the environment, and unfailing appropriate responses on the part of caregivers. However, these are ideals, and these ideals in turn are based on archetypes, on the primordial human set of intentions regarding our existence and our action in the world. Ideals are guideposts; rising from the depths of being, they can guide us consciously or unconsciously and decisively influence our goals. However, the ideal qualities with which we endow the child and childhood are qualities that belong to the divine child. The divine child can never be integrated, however; it can only be reflected in us.

Ideals become dangerous when we are possessed by them and unconsciously fixated on them. Then we become fanatical and intolerant and believe that only our opinions and attitudes count.

The person who feels full of an ideal in this way is inflated. Inflation is an overblown quality that gives the individual the misguided feeling of being more than just a human being with all the human limitations. Inflations are always based on unconscious identification with an archetypal (one might even say divine) quality. The unconscious identification with the divine child means that reality is unrecognized and qualities are constantly sought that cannot exist in life, or can exist only at certain times. The person who unconsciously strives for the divine child thinks that he has to appear naive, spontaneous, and totally natural, and does not notice how ridiculous he often appears in forcing these ideals. The present-day predilection for psychology encourages many people to talk loudly of openness and naturalness and advocate living out all their impulses. I consider it extremely important to distinguish the human element from the divine, to be aware that the divine child exceeds the human measure and earthly possibilities.

Identification with the divine child also expresses itself in the infantile shadow. If we are unconsciously identified with the divine child, we are also, to a certain extent, infantile. This means we believe in the feasibility of freedom, naturalness, harmony, innocence, and perfection, and we project these ideals onto people and situations. This leads to disappointment. A good example is the belief in progress that we all have, the belief in unlimited growth. The development of the last two decades unmistakably shows that such ideals and ill-considered convictions might soon bring about our downfall through ecological catastrophe. Because the child always means development, progress, and growth, these ideals are also the gods of our Western civilization. Unrestricted faith in them has something infantile about it. These are the gods that have clay feet; although their value for earlier times is indisputable, today they must be exposed as idols.

Making the divine child conscious means two things: first, distinguishing ourselves from the qualities attributed to it and confining ourselves to the human dimension; second, making the effort to strive for these ideals wherever possible and meaningful and recognizing them as guideposts. This two-sided approach is a contradiction, meaning yes and no at the same time. Choosing between the two is a human responsibility within the framework of the humanly possible. Living within the measure of the humanly possible is what constitutes human worth. Thus, integration of the divine child means not only limiting oneself to the humanely possible, but also developing insight into human dignity and wielding human authority.

The following dream of a man now forty years old, which recurred a number of times with variations, has to do with the infantile shadow:

> I am a child and am walking through the world at a distance
> of approximately a half meter from the ground. I glide freely
> over the earth, and between me and the ground there is a kind
> of cushion of air.

Because this dream motif was recurrent over a long period of time, we occupied ourselves with it in analysis a number of times and considered the dream image from various perspectives, until gradually the following meaning crystallized. Rainer (as I shall call the dreamer here) was unconsciously fused in his ego with an infantile shadow, which appears in the dream as a child who has no ground under his feet. It was his habitual pattern to stand above things, to hover over them. Attracted to unworldly ideals and paradisaic expectations centered on the divine child, he not only tried to fulfill them himself but also expected them from other people and situations. Identification with the divine child gave him a quality of being alienated from reality and a considerable sense of disconnectedness. For the sake of peace and harmony he often stood apart from discussions. He shied away from confrontations because he was afraid they would result in restrictions of his freedom. Thus he was never completely involved in life and also felt this to be his biggest problem. He did not know what direction to take in his life and found it difficult to relate to the idea of marriage, knowing all too well from experience that as soon as he committed himself he would feel confined and would have a strong desire to break free and set out for new horizons.

These free-floating states also naturally had their good sides and often proved helpful. Rainer was a therapist, and in looking at this dream we were both spontaneously reminded of Freud's demand for "free-floating attention" in therapy. In fact, it is essential for everyone in a therapeutic profession to be able to let his or her attention float free, so to speak, so as not to fall into the trap of rash interpretations. This ability to maintain an unprejudiced and impartial attitude was quite helpful to Rainer in working with people, and he was talented enough to make good use of it.

In a process of extending his consciousness of himself, Rainer gradually became aware of his infantile shadow. He learned to see why he was identified with it and was consequently better able to distinguish between reality and idealism, between the divine and the earthly child. Thus he was able to accept the human dimension.

THE DIVINE CHILD IN TIME OF NEED

The divine child is reflected as a holy child in the human psyche in dreams, visions, and imagination. In times of deepest inner conflict, a healing effect emanates from it, as we saw earlier in the dreams of Friedrich Huch and Sabine. I heard a follower of the Eastern Orthodox church recount how, in times of inner turmoil, he always contemplated and meditated on the icon of the Madonna and Child as an image of incarnation and of the special yet infinitely variable relationship between the human being and God.

The divine child as archetype of the Self, as I have already stated, can only be *reflected* in the human soul. Only times of crisis in our inner life allow the archetypal traits to stand out more clearly than usual.

The hallucinated child that some psychotic women believe they have borne is regarded as an expression of psychic illness. We might also mention those disturbed persons who believe themselves to be the Madonna and their child to be the child of God. In mental illness, too, sacrificial fantasies frequently center on children, and the patient might actually want to kill a child as a sacrifice. A vivid account of such a case is found in the autobiographical notes of a Swiss doctor, Domenic Gaudenz, who describes the religious delusion of a female patient as follows:

> She lived in a world of imagination and in a religious delusion. She considered herself the bride of Jesus. . . . Jesus appeared to her and promised to marry her if she would sacrifice her young daughter to him.
> One day she decorated her room magnificently; she set the table for two people. . . . She created a festive atmosphere with many, many flowers. She made herself beautiful because today the bridegroom was to come, today was her wedding day! Little Sabine, the little first-grader, came home. . . . Her mother greeted her with crazed eyes, grabbed her with the strength of one possessed, bound her, tying her arms to her body with a rope she had laid ready, and wrapped her up in it completely. Then she carried the child out to the forecourt of the house. There she had a split stick and a broad ax waiting, so that she could chop off the child's head.[18]

The poor sick woman's plan was thwarted, however, and the child was rescued. This makes clear the extent to which, in such states, threatening and destructive archetypal patterns affect consciousness and drive the ego to pathological actions and impulses.

The most impressive evidence I have found for the appearance of the archetypal pattern of mother and child in the psychic life of a healthy person was documented by Cordelia Edvardson, daughter of the poet Elisabeth Langgässer (1899–1950). Edvardson, born half Jewish, was thrown into the hell of Auschwitz in early puberty and survived. She gives an account of her difficult childhood, the time in the concentration camp, and the years afterward in a moving book whose title translates as "A Burned Child Seeks the Fire." There we find the story of a mother who was told that she could only save herself by handing her child over to be killed. The mother did not go along with the SS henchman's offer, but chose to die in the gas chamber with her child. In grasping and describing this extreme situation, Evardson uses the comparison of the Madonna with her divine child.

No pictures, no fairy tales and stories remained to comfort the girl and sustain her. The insatiable void had swallowed everything.

Instead she dwells on a picture of reality; it lured and frightened her; she hardly dared touch it, yet it was so beautiful, as full of unattainable longing as pictures of the Madonna painted on a golden background. These pictures with their miniature cities, gardens, and people living their own sheltered lives in the background of the picture are illuminated by the golden radiance of the mother and child. Yet this picture is dangerous and has to be—but cannot be—pushed away and forgotten.

And this is the girl's picture: The beautiful blond woman stands in front of Mengele or another SS man with shiny black boots. The woman holds a child pressed close to her body, the eight- to ten-year-old stands in front of her, and she has her arms wrapped around him so firmly that the two, the woman and child, seem to have grown together.

How the mother got the child into the camp at all, the girl does not know; perhaps they both came in an "unsorted" transport from Therienstadt and she was able to hide her child—for a while. The SS man appears to know the woman well. He calls her by her first name, he argues and tries to convince her, beseeches her to save her own life by handing over the child, the condemned child. The mother refuses. Finally she and the child are led by a guard through the camp gate down a straight path to the gas chamber. The woman holds the child's hand, she walks upright, bending only now and again to say something to the child. There is still so much to say and the child trots along trustingly, not struggling, not seeming to have any fear. Perhaps the mother is telling him about the "little bird seeking protection under its mother's wings and the child resting securely in its mother's lap."[19]

In this moment the mother and her child lived the divine pattern to the very edge of the possible and, anonymous among the many victims, have become superb witnesses to the power of human action in the light of the divine and in the shadow of extremity.

4 The Child of God

I STILL vividly recall from my childhood the sayings of older members of my family, who spoke the words "child of God" again and again with varying emphasis. "Child of God" could be a tender expression of love; however, spoken emphatically, "child of God" also expressed a certain resigned surrender on the part of the adults in the face of my naughtiness. Years later the deep significance of these words struck me, and I had to think back nostalgically on my childhood days when my grandmother and great-aunts used this meaningful expression as a matter of course. Feeling oneself to be a child of God is something beautiful. The words evince God's unconditional affection for His creation, as in the words "Think of the love that the Father has lavished on us, by letting us be called God's children; and that is what we are" (1 John 3:1). The person who is granted faith in this experiences existential certainty.

However, such fundamental certainty is granted to few people, and many people have an image of God as punitive and vengeful. Taught absolute obedience to their parents, they have also built up an image of God according to which they owe God the Father a reckoning for all their actions as well as unconditional obedience. Such a God image, it seems to me, is a parent complex carried over into the suprapersonal realm and does not have much to do with God and religious experience. The image of a punitive God, which finds its parallel in the absolute obedience of children to their parents, is historically based. It began to spread at the start of the modern era, mostly through the teachings of Martin Luther, which were unfortunately misconstrued.[1] The old hierarchical structures of the Middle Ages had collapsed, and new ones had to be found. Thus was adopted a ladder of obedience on the lowest rung of which stood the children and on the highest the parents, teachers, and priests. Each was to serve the next higher with obedience and submissiveness. This schema required a retributive and omnipresent God who concerns Himself with every offense. The rod rather than love and affection was the suitable instrument for dealing with children. "Beat the boy regularly; thus you will gain his respect," said the pedagogue Hans Sachs, a contemporary of Luther.[2]

This educational theory, accurately characterized by Katharina Rutschky as "black pedagogy," has been preserved through the generations on into our time. The short story "The Stubborn Child," published by the Grimms although already referred to three hundred years earlier in Hans Sachs's *Treatise on Disciplining Children* (1552), describes a child upon whom God sends sickness and death as a punishment for its stubbornness. From this and similar sources, one can infer to what extent God was seen as retributive and vengeful. In this context, the child of God is seen as obedient and willing to fit in. The original concept of the child of God redolent with a sense of God's unconditional love has been turned into its opposite: only one who is good and pious and serves heaven through obedience and good works is a child of God.

The person who can free himself from this sense of virtue through achievement, who can find his way to an innocent sense of trust and thus feel himself to be a child of God in the original positive sense of being unconditionally accepted—that person is granted the gift of childlike faith or receives the grace of a new emotional orientation.

THE LOSS OF CHILDLIKE FAITH

One of the first dreams reported by a woman named Inge who was in analysis with me involved her having fallen asleep during the session and having hummed to herself like a child:

> I was at Mrs. Asper's. Suddenly I asked her, "Did I fall asleep?" She said yes. I thought, What's going on here? Me with nervous, hyperactive style, falling asleep in analysis?

> She said I had had my eyes closed and was softly humming or making a droning sound. I thought—still in the dream—that that had been my way when I was a child. I always used to hum and sing softly to myself when I was quite tired.

In connection with this dream, another dream scene occurred to Inge that she had dreamed two or three months previously:

> I am singing in a dream: "Let your poor child rest at your feet; it just wants to close its eyes and believe."

The dreams appeared to be about lost childhood happiness and faith. Months later they became important in Inge's analysis as the point of departure for a reawakened yearning for religious experience. But what had happened in the meantime?

Inge appeared to me to be an extremely vivacious person; she could always find something to talk about, and spoke in an interesting and enjoyable way. In the telling, her memories acquired a sense of charming excitement. I enjoyed listening to her and felt invigorated by it. The way Inge talked also had something breathless and disjointed about it, though, and I had to ask questions frequently so as not to lose the thread. She often digressed and lost track of why she had touched on this or that subject.

In pondering Inge's way of filling up the hours in analysis and my own reaction to this, the picture arose of an overeager little child who constantly has to assure herself of the presence and well-being of her mother and other family members, is constantly on the alert to please everyone, and tries to cheer up everybody around her. I shared this impression with Inge and asked her if it was true that she had behaved that way as a child. That had actually been the case. Inge was the much-longed-for only child of relatively old parents. Her grandmother, an unmarried aunt, and an unmarried uncle had been living in the same household. From the very beginning she was the focal point; the attention of the whole family was directed toward the little girl. Inge was not only pretty but also quite a talented child, and soon became the object of the hopes, yearnings, and wishes of her parents, as well as of her aunt, uncle, and grand-

mother. Tragic events of war, poverty, and difficult circumstances had characterized the life of the adults around Inge.
None of them still expected much from life, but they all hoped
for much from the child and assigned to her the retrieval of the
family's honor.

Inge had been born into a milieu of deep faith. The members
of the family, who frequently quarreled with each other, found
themselves united in a sense of pietistic religiosity. Their strong
faith was the source from which they drew strength, and the
child was their joy, hope, and the promise of a better future.

Inge quickly and willingly accepted the secret message that
came to her from her family. She had been given the role of
making her relatives happy, especially her mother, who had
been disappointed by life. The role also included making peace
when conflicts and frictions arose. It also included getting training and developing her intelligence so as to raise the family's
social position. Thus it was no wonder that Inge was constantly
trying to please everyone and to keep the people around her in
a good mood. Now as an adult she was still trying to entertain
everyone, even me during analysis. How frantically she had to
use gesture, facial expression, and speech to avoid disappoint-
ing others and to continue to fulfill the hopes that had long ago
been invested in her. Especially for her mother, Inge had represented a source of consolation. We could even safely say that
in a certain sense the roles had been reversed and that Inge had
at times mothered her mother.

A key memory involved a minor but highly typical scene.
During the war, when Inge, a five-year-old at the time, was
fleeing with her mother, the latter became seriously ill, so seriously that she thought she was going to die. In her concern she
shared her situation with Inge, and Inge—she still remembered
this quite clearly—said, "Don't worry, I still have my aunt!"
This statement, as funny as it might have sounded from a child's
mouth, is actually deeply sad. When Inge said this to her
mother, she comforted her first and did not think about her own
sadness and fear. As a child she could comfort others so well
and fulfill the role that had been imposed on her of providing

sunshine and being a symbol of hope, because she had an undisturbed childlike faith in a good heavenly father. Inge experienced herself as a child in the true sense as a "child of God," accepted and loved unconditionally. God was her mother and father at the same time; from Him the child innocently and naturally drew strength, courage, comfort, and security in life.

The dreams described above became completely understandable against the background of these childhood memories. Inge falling asleep in the dream during the analysis session and softly humming to herself and Inge singing the pious song of childlike faith in the other dream—this Inge no longer existed in adult life. This childlike faithfulness had been shattered and lost, but as an adult, Inge longed to return to it, and rightly so. Her longing, ultimately, was for inner peace and a psychological-spiritual home in the religious sense. Her two short dreams were of great importance for this reason and had already quite precisely introduced at the beginning of the process the theme that was to be central to her whole analysis. They had harked back to her childhood, but they had heralded the future too.

As a result of the spiritual atmosphere in her parents' house, Inge had studied theology, thus fulfilling her family's desire for higher status. But at the same time she had lost her faith, and it had not been granted her to be able to develop her genuine childlike faith into an equally genuine mature faith. This increased her inner restlessness. She sought spiritual nourishment and devoured book after book, filled with enthusiasm for other spiritual paths, then turned away from them disappointed, and set out to realize other aspirations. Her keen intelligence permitted her to make her way easily in the spiritual realm and to acquire considerable knowledge.

What Inge lacked, however, was the ability to relate to herself and to take her own thoughts and feelings seriously. Just as she had once set the members of her family above herself and not taken her own feelings and thoughts into account, she now still considered the opinions and pronouncements of her spiritual teachers, models, and acquaintances more important than her own thoughts and impulses. Someone who has to fulfill such a barrage of unconscious demands from her environment as a child finds it difficult to get away from them later. This was true for Inge, too. For that reason the following dream was promising and favorable, because it involved Inge's wanting to pay more attention to herself. Though it is not a dream in which a child appears, it vividly portrays the attitude, which had become second nature to her in her adult life, of satisfying others before attending to her own needs.

> I was in a store and tried on a bikini and jackets. Everything fit all right but not stunningly. Again and again I tried on three jackets and almost bought one of them. But finally I said to the saleslady, a somewhat older lady, that I preferred not to buy anything, but it would be embarrassing for me after having taken up so much of her time. However, she said to me in a quite friendly way, "But it goes without saying that you can just forget it. That is our job." And in confidence she said to me that there were better, larger clothing stores where I would have a larger selection. I was surprised. Pleased, I went away.
>
> For the first time I hadn't taken something out of a sense of propriety, but rather postponed my purchase. Besides, I also wanted a nice bright jacket, cream or white, which would go with fashionable summer things. I could look for it somewhere else.

In a figurative sense Inge had "purchased" again and again the ideas and opinions of other people. Thus she had allowed too little expression of her own reactions. She let too much be imposed on her and hardly allowed herself to become aware of her own thoughts, which, if they ever got to be formulated and heard, were good and original. Here in the dream she did not, as in the past, buy something that only half fit, but decided to find the jacket that appealed to her.

So then, in analysis, we also looked into this "jacket" of her own. What it meant was that which was her own: her own thoughts, feelings, fantasies, and impulses. The more Inge centered herself, the calmer she became. She is still on the way to herself, but already the first signs of a changed experience of herself and the world are becoming noticeable. As she began taking the history of her childhood seriously, her memories of her child-like faith were also awakened. Linked to this, the longing for a new understanding of faith and religious experience flickered to life . Where yearning begins to stir, hope is always there as well. For Inge this meant hope for a new encounter with God.

THE FILIAL RELATIONSHIP TO GOD

A man whom I will call Alex, who had already passed midlife and was in his fifty-fifth year, had the following dream in the second year of analysis:

> I am walking along a dark corridor; on the right and left are doors at regular intervals. Ahead is an indescribable light which floods everything. The light is not an ordinary but a supernatural one. It inspires me and makes me blissful and streams out toward me. Deeply moved, I say the words "Father, father, have you come?" An inner feeling I had never known before of being accepted just as I am arose in me. It is the feeling of being allowed to be, with all my inconsistencies.

The dreamer experienced himself as a son in this dream, as a child of God, affirmed and accepted. This experience was new for him, because up to this point his life had proceeded along well-ordered paths, for which the somewhat dark corridor in the dream, strictly subdivided by doors, was a striking image. His whole life long, he had always tried to please everyone and thus had eagerly and conscientiously undertaken tasks and had carried them out in such a way that they benefitted not only his family but also his professional field. Others saw him as a typical leader, as fatherly, even patriarchal, in a positive sense. People turned to him for advice and asked him for help in times of need. He never refused these requests and favors. His lifestyle as well as his understanding of himself and the world were based on high ideals, values such as fulfillment of duty, objectivity, truth, and love of others. Alex constantly tried to put the needs of others before his own, and this service to others gave his life meaning. In brief, he led a virtuous life.

Looking at his personality from a psychological viewpoint, we see that he had strongly identified himself with patriarchal Christian moral concepts throughout his life, and as a result the paternal element had begun to mold his character more and more one-sidedly. If we ask how this happened, much can be said, covering the whole spectrum from basic makeup to environment. Striking in Alex's development was that, from the very beginning of his life, there were always people, situations, and periods of time that demanded a paternal, guiding and duty-oriented behavior from him. In his strictly religious parental household, these values were instilled in him by his parents in a matter-of-course, unquestioned way.

As the oldest and also a quite talented son, he had to set an example for his younger siblings; later he had to take on a role of brotherly guidance toward his handicapped younger brother and was appointed his guardian. During the critical years of the 1930s his father had been forced to earn a living far away from the family. As a result of his father's absence, Alex spontaneously grew into the role of masculine head of the family. Later he wanted to go to college, being a brilliant young man, but his parents could not afford to pay for his studies. Nonetheless he enrolled at the university, applied for a scholarship, and in addition earned his living through hard work, for example, as a waiter in the student cafeteria. Thus at a time when others could enjoy their youth and studies, Alex undertook responsibility not only for his studies but also for his livelihood. It goes without saying that this situation forced Alex into the position of an outsider. Compelled by circumstances, he developed a lifestyle far more mature than that of his fellow students. Nevertheless he was popular, but welcomed less as an equal than as a helper and fatherly or brotherly friend.

His readiness to react paternally may well have been a part of his basic makeup, which then, conditioned by environmental factors, led to a strong inclination to develop paternal qualities at the expense of other attributes. From the perspective of Jung's analytical psychology, we can say that Alex's life was strongly determined by the father archetype, which means that the paternal potentialities of his psyche had been excessively developed. His father complex was a positive one in contrast to Bernhard's (discussed in chapter 1). This overemphasis of the patriarchal attitude, although it operated positively, led to Alex's identifying too much with the Great Father archetype; as a result, other qualities were relegated to the shadow: spontaneity, naturalness, and feelings and emotions. His self-image was codified in terms of patriarchal ideals, and opposing impulses and tendencies were always pushed aside. He did not allow himself, and gradually became unable, to be himself in all his naturalness and spontaneity. He had distanced himself from his natural roots and invested too much in his persona. In analytical psychology, *persona* refers to the face that we show to the world, as well as the many-sided aspects of relating to the outside world. Alex ended up emphasizing his persona too much at the cost of other kinds of expression. He had "forcibly separated himself from his original character in favor of an involuntary persona suitable for ambition" and had become "unchildlike and artificial" and lost "his roots."[3]

It was primarily Alex's dreams that drew attention to this one-sided orientation. From the very beginning of the analysis, they pointed toward the other sides of him and called his patriarchal orientation into question. It was not until the dream about the light, cited above, that Alex began to be aware of his identification with the persona and patriarchal values. In this dream he experienced at a deep emotional level the feeling of being accepted as a child of God. This touches upon what theologians refer to as the filial relationship with God.[4] This idea is an ancient one, found also outside of Christianity. What is new in the message of Jesus is the great closeness between God and His creation. The individual can address God familiarly, as "Father," and even with the term of endearment *Abba* (Mark 14:36). The filial relationship to God is ultimately one of grace and includes the forgiveness of all sins, because God "maketh his sun to rise on the evil and on the good, and sendeth rain on the just and the unjust" (Matt. 5:45). Thus it involves the immediate presence of God in the sense expressed in the idea that everyone is held in the Father's hand (Ps. 139). The benevolent father side of God shows above all in His behavior toward the prodigal son (Luke 15:11 ff.). When the son comes home and asks for forgiveness, his father greets him in a manner that might well be described as maternal. He embraces him, puts a ring on his finger, has him fitted with new clothing, and arranges for a great celebration. No word of reproach is spoken, nor is mention made of sin and repentance. He simply welcomes his son and is happy that he who was "dead" is "alive again."

The original message of the filial relationship to God as something that simply *exists* without conditions, was soon changed by dogma into something reserved for only the pious, well-behaved, virtuous, and just—the doers of good works. This is exactly what happened to Alex. He only felt accepted if he was constantly achieving, being responsible, and putting out effort. Thus what he experienced in the dream was the miracle of being accepted without works, the rediscovery of Jesus' original message that one *is* a child of God just as one is. But for Alex, the idea of being as one is without contrivance contained the difficult step of accepting and being accepted. Less instead of more was expected of him now, and he repeatedly reverted to the old attitude of having to achieve in order to be accepted. The message of the dream was ultimately the need to rediscover the earthy child. In the dream, overwhelmed by light, he speaks the words "Father, father have you come?" Very deep inside, he experienced himself as a son, and for the first time differentiated himself from the father role he had played his whole life.

His dream reminded me of the conversation about rebirth between Jesus and Nicodemus, in which Jesus says: "I tell you most solemnly, unless a man is born from above, he cannot see the kingdom of God" (John 3:3). And: "I tell you most solemnly, unless a man is born through water and the Spirit, he cannot enter the kingdom of God" (John 3:5). The questioning cry in the dream—"Father, father, have you come?"—seems to me connected to the experience of rebirth "from above" that Jesus described. In the dream state Alex in a certain sense experienced a rebirth that had a liberating effect on his future self-understanding. From that point on, he could be not only the father but also the son.

Starting with this dream, something happened to Alex. The change expressed itself first in an altered view of himself. He became aware of his identification with the father archetype, noticed that he had ignored his own feelings and emotions in deference to it, and was increasingly able to accept other perspectives. Something mischievous began to come out in him, along with greater naturalness and a willingness to tolerate imperfections. Shadow aspects were emerging. His childlike side, his spontaneity and naturalness, which had been living in the shadow up to this point, were demanding to come to light. Immediately following the light dream came two other significant dreams:

> I am in a rowboat. Another man sits in the boat with me. He moves the boat in a spiteful way, almost making me fall out. But now I make the boat rock and get a big kick out of seeing the man fall headfirst into the water.

> A severe storm has broken out. The ships and boats moored in the harbor pitch and toss ominously back and forth alarmingly in the high waves. The storm wind blows through the leaves and trees, the branches creak, a large branch breaks. I am directly in the line of the fall, and the branch threatens to hit me. Yet I am unmoved by the danger. I simply walk somewhat faster and continue on my way unwaveringly. I am carrying a briefcase in my hand.

If he is childish in the first dream, in the second he is completely the opposite, a thoroughly masculine adult. But let's look more closely! Alex understood the second dream in the sense that despite emotional storms and inner turmoil he remained calm according to his ideal of being above things and being brave. He realized that the dream was showing him his lifelong attitude and called attention to how one-sidedly unwavering he had become.

In connection with this, many small situations occurred to him in which he had behaved in an exclusively masculine and unwavering fashion. He remembered a dinner during which a woman had reacted to his remarks in an inexplicably irritable way, treating him to a number of sharp comments. The conversation revolved around the roles of the sexes and the many emotional entanglements between men and women. Alex participated in the conversation but tried to smooth the waters (!) and said with sustained emphasis: "We all need each other." This quickly brought down on him one of the barbed comments of his dinner companion. Although it could be that the woman reacted negatively because she was in a bad mood, more than likely what happened was this: There was a lively discussion going on in which the participants were subjectively involved on an emotional level. Alex tried to raise this to another, more objective level and set a schoolmasterish truism in its place. He had become a father and spoken with an air of instruction. In this context, his dinner companion's angry reaction becomes completely understandable. Probably a response in which he talked about himself and his own feelings, using "I" statements, would have been received quite differently. Just as in his dream, Alex had wanted to regard the troubled waters from above and had proceeded on his unwavering path.

In the first of the two dreams above, the mischievous side of Alex comes out. He reacts spontaneously and in a humorously aggressive way and makes his nasty companion fall into the water. Instead of acting according to his ideals here, he immediately responds with an action that does not fit in with his usual values. A spontaneous childish side, in the shadow up to this point, asserts itself in the dream. Alex, who at first morally condemned his behavior in the dream, soon began to feel pleased about it. In this connection, he had dreams similar to the two below and came to understand what they signified.

> I am walking on water and do not sink.
>
> I am cooking dinner for friends. In a magical way, solely through the power of will, I can warm the food and even produce food, but I do not let the others see this. That would be going too far.

Both dreams show Alex identified with the healer and helper archetype. Jesus can walk on water without sinking, and only

Jesus can increase the amount of food so that it is enough for the feeding of the five thousand (Matt. 14:21). The person who succumbs to such an identification, rather than being childlike, has abandoned the human measure. For Alex it was an ideal to be a helper. However, these dreams showed him that he was identifying with the helper archetype and its corresponding attitudes. The light dream, with its profound experience of being accepted by a father, initiated, as could be seen in retrospect, a development of personality that allowed Alex to separate himself from the Great Father, to accept his childlike aspects, and to live and tolerate the human dimension and imperfections. A twisted dogmatic Christianity could be gradually discarded in favor of freer attitudes. Alex became new in the sense that he could recognize his shadow aspects. The dream experience and the subsequent confrontation with it helped him to feel increasingly alive and to make room for the concept of the filial relationship to God in its original content.

In pondering over Alex and his development, an unconscious assumption of my own came liberatingly to light. Alex, who in the dreams sees the light and has the experience of being accepted, experienced the divine not as choosing him and making him important, but rather as an affirmation of his human existence with all its shadow aspects. The experience of the light as an epiphany of the divine neither assigned him a task nor demanded anything special from him. On the contrary, in this brief dream moment he had the deep existential experience of being affirmed as a human being just as he was. The theologian Paul Tillich describes this gracious affirmation with the following lines:

> Sometimes in such a moment a ray of light breaks into our darkness, and it is as though a voice has spoken: You are accepted, accepted by one who is greater than you and whose name you do not know. Do not ask the name now; perhaps later you will learn it. Do not try to do anything; perhaps later you will do much. Seek nothing; achieve nothing. Simply accept the fact that you are accepted.[5]

This experience guided Alex away from striving for perfection and achievement. It afforded him a deeper understanding of his shadow and called upon him to bring the unexperienced or hardly experienced sides of himself more and more into his life. This experience confirmed the importance of seeking personal completeness rather than perfection. The shadow—the dark parts of the personality and the possibilities that have not been realized—is essential to completeness. The path to which the light dream urged him was, in visual terms, no longer one that was to lead him to the heights, but rather quite definitely one whose goal was breadth. For Alex this meant being no longer godlike but human, which for him meant a revaluation of all values. The event in the dream affirmed precisely the human, the human imperfection in himself as willed by God. This was a message that was previously unknown to him and stood in contrast to the Christian view he had grown up with, according to which only "better and better" and "more and more perfect" were pleasing to God.

The experience of being a son connected him increasingly to the child in himself, the child he once had been and from whose condition of wholeness he had become distant. This child, however, also pointed toward the future and intimated a renewal of personality. The child was the carrier of his Self, his own inner nature. Jung says about such a child: "It represents the strongest and most unavoidable impulse of nature, actualizing oneself."[6] Self-actualization in this new sense means contacting our buried childlike possibilities, allowing ourselves to become more natural and increasingly leaving behind the paternal aspect of ourselves.

5 The Smiling Child

NOTHING about children charms the hearts of adults more than their smiles. The smiling child is the embodiment of carefreeness and harmony with oneself and the world; yet this also is ultimately a projection of divine qualities onto the actual child. Divine children smile.

In Vergil's *Eclogues*, the most noted source of pre-Christian belief in a saviour, the child smiles and attests to his divine origin. "Now, little boy, give your mother a friendly laugh to show her that you know her. You should know that only from people who have given their mother a friendly laugh does God choose his table companions and a goddess her bed companions."[1] In the understanding at that time, (c. 40 B.C.), the child's smile was regarded as divine because people believed that children do not laugh until the fortieth day of life.[2] This belief survived for centuries. It is also reflected in superstition, where the actual child's smile is regarded with distrust and is not considered human. Only miraculous and divine children laugh right after birth, or they become mute or stutter. Children who smile early are suspected as demons or have a serious illness in store.[3] Only much later did the idea, still widespread today, develop that the child smiling in its sleep is in contact with angels who are saying something friendly into its ear.

The Christ Child's smile is also linked to his divinity and his divine origin. However, ultimately his smile is precious and special, because laughing just does not play an important role in the whole of Christology, and Christianity is humorless in general. We never hear about the three leading figures—God the Father, Mary, and Jesus—laughing, certainly not laughing heartily nor bringing forth any kind of golden humor. We have to turn to folk literature and the apocryphal (not canonized) writings to find traces of humor in Christianity. The high-spirited boy Jesus, who is devoid of all wish to be helpful and is something of a mischief maker, plays an important role, for example, in the childhood stories in the Gospel of Thomas. The famous legends, according to which Jesus made birds out of clay, are not without humor and pranks: Jesus, at the age of five, was playing with other children beside a river on the Sabbath, and he made some birds from the soft clay. One of the children reported the Sabbath violation to Joseph. When Joseph took his son to task for this, Jesus clapped his hands and shouted to the birds, "Away with you!" and the birds, which were still just clay, flew away squawking.[4] The scene is often portrayed at this moment, with the birds flying away from Jesus as a smile shows on his face; his playmates' birds do not move, and their faces reflect their envy and disappointment. The scene directly communicates its sense of mischief, and Jesus appears full of the joy and zest for life. Of course the deeper meaning is that the bird symbolizes the human soul, and it is granted to Jesus to lead people to an encounter with their own living souls.

Folk literature is rich in stories about holy figures and also shows them from their humorous side. The stories make us laugh, thus balancing out for Christianity's persistently serious tone. There is a Provençal legend about two kinds of laughter, the demonic and the triumphant. Saint Joseph leaves his carpenter shop for a short time one day. A demon comes in and makes notches in the cutting edge of a large knife. Then he hides so he can gloat over Joseph's rage. Joseph actually does fly into a rage, which is answered by the demon's hideous laughter. But then Joseph looks at the things more closely and starts cutting with the notched knife, and "*ritsch-ratsch, ritsch-ratsch,*" the wood cuts better than before, because the knife has become a saw. Now Joseph laughs triumphantly: he who laughs last, laughs best![5]

The smile, recognized early as a characteristic quality of the divine child, is often now attributed to real children as an essential natural feature. The regressive paradise fantasies of care-laden adults flow down upon the smiling child, the pledge of our lost innocence. Doubtless children do smile, and indeed children do have a delightful way of laughing. But if we glorify children on that account, we attribute a divine quality to them; we endow them with a trait that in its purity is fitting only for the gods. Projections distort reality. Children are not only sweet, smiling little angels; perfidious laughter at others is a prominent feature of children as well.

A projection can be constricting for the person upon whom it is cast. Children who repeatedly hear that they should make a happy face are stuck with this their whole lives. The smile finally becomes a defense mechanism that conceals feelings that are not approved. With this mechanism, the child (and later the adult) also puts himself under the protection of those who accept and affirm him because of his friendly face.

I am reminded of a middle-aged woman whose mother used to quote lines from an operetta, *The Land of Smiles*, when faced with adverse circumstances: "Smile, always just smile. . . ." She also offered these words to her child when difficult feelings arose for her—for instance, after an admonition from her teacher or the loss of a beloved pet. The child wanted to be heard in her rage and pain, but her mother tossed these words at her in singsong tones, thus demanding an unwholesome bravery from the child. It turns out that children treated in this way lose trust in their own feelings. They start to consider their feelings wrong and become accustomed to suppressing them. In so doing they lose a good deal of their capacity to experience feelings and liveliness. But a smile is shown to the world.

The following short dream of a man, whom I shall call Beat, shows how such a split in one's emotional life can occur.

> Two boys are in a room. One is dressed up as an Indian, the other as a clown. They are playing carnival. The mother comes in, is outraged by the mess, and immediately starts to scold. The Indian child draws his knife, the clown child smiles at the mother. The mother turns toward the clown child, takes him by the hand, and leaves the room with him. The Indian child stays behind, angry, raging, and sad.

This dreams shows a key scene from Beat's childhood and depicts with diagnostic insight the origin of his neurosis. His mother preferred the smiling, laughing, cheerful side of him and rejected so-called negative emotions such as anger, rage, fear, and sadness. She did this by changing the subject, soothing the feeling away, or punishing, but mostly through the example of her own effort to repress unpleasant emotions. The Indian lad, with his violence and aggressiveness, was, as in the dream, neither recognized nor accepted by his mother and consequently remained in the background. However, she confirmed the little clown, and Beat grasped quickly that he could "get along" better this way, could gain rewards as well as his mother's love. In this way, a split in his emotional life developed. It caused Beat to begin to hold back unapproved feelings and to smile. In the course of the years he developed a constant stereotyped smile that became second nature. It was very difficult for him to get rid of this, and his spontaneity and true feelings suffered.

The demand that we smile in a friendly way and fit in ultimately fosters a depressive way of processing events. I am referring to the unconscious behavior of always blaming oneself first, even when there is better reason to criticize others. This depressive processing is the opposite of the "grandiose" approach, in which one's negative aspects are camouflaged by a grandiose self-glorifying style and the blame is laid on others.

Adrian, a forty-eight-year-old theologian, had the tendency to take life seriously and readily blamed himself for difficulties. A dream clearly showed up this behavior.

> Someone has made me angry. I go into my pantry and pee there. Outside, a brass band marches by, and I hear music very clearly.

Instead of defending himself, Adrian withdraws, closes himself in his pantry, and urinates, which means that he defiles the provisions that figuratively stand for his own worth and potential. The dream very clearly shows Adrian's tendency toward criticizing and soiling himself rather than taking into account the other's possible mistake and defending himself accordingly.

This behavior had its origin in his childhood, when his parents, through excessive training of conscience, encouraged their children always to seek blame in themselves first. Aggression was frowned upon and had to be warded off with a friendly smile. The march music in the dream suggested another way of behaving. It meant for Adrian, in dealing with such circumstances, to drop the brooding, the excessive self-recrimination, and march forward in a lively way.

In this example we can see that the smile can be misused as a manipulative way of training obedience. It leads to suppressing impulses essential to life to the detriment of one's development toward wholeness.

HAPPY CHILDREN

Happiness, playfulness, and radiant optimism are other qualities of the child that are emphasized. These traits are portrayed very clearly in children's books. For example, there is Pippi Longstocking, the cheerful heroine who is always up to pranks in the series of children's novels by the Swedish children's author Astrid Lindgren. If we go back further in history, we find Max and Moritz (Or Max and Morris, as they are called in the English version), Wilhelm Busch's (1832–1908) youthful heroes who are tireless, disobedient, always ready for a prank and a laugh. Max and Moritz may be considered the first rebels against a century-long educational philosophy of suppression and forced obedience. Indeed their creator pays due reverence to the educational style of this time, introducing their seven boyish tricks with the words:

> Oh, what one often must hear
> Or read about bad children!
> For example, these two here,
> Who are called Max and Moritz.
> Who, instead of mending their ways
> Through wise teaching,
> Often laughed at it instead
> And secretly mocked it.
> "Yes, we are out to do mischief!"

Teasing people, tormenting animals,
Stealing apples, pears, plums—
That is surely more pleasant
And easier too
Than being stuck on a chair
In church or in school.
But woe, woe, woe,
When I see the outcome!
Oh, that was a terrible thing,
How it went for Max and Moritz.
That is why what they did
Is written here for all to read.[6]

At the end they actually die, and Busch writes: "Thank God
their evil fun / Is finally done!"[7] And how they die! They are
ground to meal and scattered to the chickens as food. With this,
Busch paid his dues to the thinking of his time. That having
been done, nothing more stands in the way of Max and Moritz's
mischief. They burst all restraints, harrying the widow Bolte,
the tailor Bock, the teacher Lampel, Uncle Fritz, Master Baker,
the farmer Mecke—the whole stuck-in-the-mud community.
They run riot for the delighted reader, pouring out all the pranks
and riotous dirty tricks of generations of suppressed children.
The work would not have achieved the success it has through the
years if it did not touch all the suppressed sides of adults that
come out in it, an orgy of fun and happiness, all neatly wrapped
between two book covers. But mostly Max and Moritz delighted
children, boldly fulfilling all their forbidden desires and providing an outlet for the practical jokester in them.

It looks quite different in the case of Heinrich Hoffmann's
Struwwelpeter (1847), published in English as *Slovenly Peter*.
Hoffmann, a doctor, created this book for his oldest son and his
young patients to make the time in the waiting room pass more
quickly. The book became a great success and remains so today.
Here, though, prevailing educational views are paid more definite homage than in Busch's stories. The thumb-sucker Konrad
has his thumb cut off; the fidgeter is buried under the tablecloth
and the dishes. Little Pauline, who plays with a lighter, is burnt
alive. The children who laugh at the Moors are finally dipped in

the inkwell by big Niklas and end up darker than the darkest Negro.

Hoffmann's strongly moralizing pedagogical tone is apparent throughout. But why has this book marched triumphantly through all the nurseries? Probably not because of its moralizing alone. Its success probably has more to do with the fact that Hoffmann knew how to exaggerate the scenes in such a way that even the serious disciplinary measures have a comic effect.[8] One thinks of Konrad's mother with her yellow parasol, her little hat, and her Sunday crinoline, speaking in her old-fashioned way. "Konrad," says the good mother, "I'm going out and you are staying here"—which became quite a familiar quotation. No, children could and still can identify with Slovenly Peter. Boldly he stood there on the cover with his long frizzy hair, legs spread apart, chest inflated, arms extended, and with fingernails whose length would probably be listed in the *Guinness Book of Records* today.

If we compare Slovenly Peter to the educational wisdom of his time, as can be found in the children's books of our grandparents—I am thinking of the famous *Staubs Kinderbüchlein* ("Staub's Book for Children," first edition, 1843)—it becomes quite clear how much Slovenly Peter was a rebel. Despite very drastic punishment, he could no longer hide his roguish, villainous side. A thoroughly happy child confronts the reader in Hoffmann's creation. He is no longer inclined to pray like this:

> Give Father and Mother
> Everything good in the world;
> Let me remain good and obedient,
> As it pleases my parents.[9]

He will hardly take the following saying to heart either:

> "I want to be obedient, pious
> and industrious today and every day.
> Daily I will say to myself:
> "Keep your heart as pure as an angel's."[10]

The prayer for passing school exams does not fit in Slovenly Peter's world either. Here the children pray, are pious and good, and wouldn't hurt a hair on anyone's head:

> Our test is over,
> Diligence brings luck and blessing,
> Thankfully we clasp our hands together
> To you, O God, in praise.
>
> Our joyful hours in school,
> The springtime of our youth
> You have fashioned into a wreath;
> You, O God of glory, splendor.
>
> May each therefore strive,
> Struggle toward perfection!
> Since our life on earth
> Is the time of learning for our soul.
>
> May each calmly stand before you
> On that great judgment day
> And joyfully await
> The father's solemn question.[11]

It was only a short step from the late-nineteenth-century rebels to the "century of the child," as the Swedish pedagogue Ellen Kay has described our time.

Only a narrow rift still separated us from anti-authoritarian education, when the cartoonist, writer, and artist Friedrich Karl Waechter drew and painted his *Anti-Struwwelpeter* in 1970. This little book is a witty jab at the original *Struwwelpeter*, which teaches children the joy of disobedience and insolently laughs at strict adults. The "tailor with the mole" does not succeed in cutting off Konrad's thumb. Konrad and his young friends hold a "thumb lollipop" celebration:

> Each one sits down and
> *Whoomph!* puts his thumb in his mouth.
> Later it's cigarettes,
> It's pleasure in bed,
> But little girls and boys
> Want to feast on their thumbs.[12]

They thwart the tailor's plan to capture them in advance. When they grease the floor with soap the disciplinarian slips, falls down, and even loses his trousers!

> When Mother comes home,
> The tailor looks sad.

> He stands there without his trousers,
> And the two of them are gone.[13]

Today we view the joyous sides of children, their pranks and tomfoolery, less suspiciously and have become more tolerant in general. Children are even allowed to be joyous and contrary now. Because we also recognize valuable attempts at autonomy in these impulses, we no longer chastise children as drastically as before, when people still believed they had to control the devil himself in the child's nature.

Nevertheless, we saw in the previous section on the laughter of children how the spontaneous sides of the child can be repressed, and the educator—like the mother in Beat's dream—takes only the brave, friendly child along and leaves the other behind.

Obedience training takes place early, in infancy. Although this practice has changed considerably in our time, it still frequently happens that mothers—true to the teaching of their mothers and grandmothers—let babies cry through the night and pick them up and calm them only according to the feeding schedule. There must be order, even from the very beginning, or else children might get accustomed to privileges that would encourage bad character traits. People still do not trust the child's nature and take the position, held for centuries, that children, even as they came from the Creator's hand, are bestial, crude, and corrupt, and only education and training can make upright human beings out of them. So we let babies just cry, consider their crying contrariness, and thus forget that the child's nature often knows better than we do what its needs are.

A woman who is now sixty-five repeatedly dreamed of crying infants:

> An infant is crying in a dark room. He is blue already. I can't do anything.

The method of upbringing described above was used on this woman. She was left to cry, but it did not stop there. Even when she was older, her needs were still seldom acknowledged. Consequently she developed a faulty connection with her own impulses and not only overlooked all of her own needs but also became unable to participate fully in her joyous, happy side. The infant in the dream cries itself blue, and the dreamer succinctly goes on, "I cannot do anything." The child in the dream represents not only the baby she once was but also all of the needs in herself that she could not satisfy and that she repeatedly ignored throughout her life. As we were treated, so we frequently treat ourselves. This is so simple, yet it is very difficult to break through these internalized attitudes and just treat ourselves well, allowing ourselves to enjoy life.

Erna, who is fifty years old, dreamed about a child who was enjoying sliding back and forth on a bench and was brutally beaten by her father.

> A small girl is sitting astride a bench without a back rest and slides with pleasure from one end to the other again and again. Her father forbids her to do that. And when the child does not obey, he beats her brutally. The child tries it again and again. The father becomes more and more brutal. Now it is no longer punishment but rather rage, which the child resists. I watch, not understanding why the child should not play; I'm appalled by the senseless cruelty and about the fact that I feel helpless and do not intervene.

Laughter is disappearing for this child, and her sense of enjoyment is being thoroughly knocked out of her. But the punishment, hard to justify in the first place, was not the end of the matter. The act of punishment changed into blind fury and helpless rage. The dreamer, though very upset, felt helpless in the face of this outbreak and did not intervene. What is shown in the dream is frequently observed in reality. The reason why children are punished is often not that they committed some offense; rather, it is because the parents, owing to their own internalized parent figures see in the child all those sides of themselves that they were not allowed to live out. Their unconscious motto is, "What I was not permitted, you will not be permitted either." The child who touches upon their own mischievous and forbidden sides also instills fear in the adult, because parental figures from their own childhood are still internally at work. The person who hits a child often does so out of unconscious fear of punishment.

Finally, we have to consider the reversal of roles. A violent parent is often releasing all his still-unconscious fury against his own parents; the rage that he could not show his father and mother is now unleashed on his own child, who becomes the suitable object for bottled-up feelings of hatred. The parent lashes out freely, without fear of retaliation. Thus, ultimately, the furious adult is hitting his own parents in his child. This complicated intertwining of relationships can at least in part explain the helpless fury that, unfortunately, we frequently see in parents toward their own children.

Because of her strict upbringing, Erna had lost her capacity for laughter and enjoyment. The spontaneous, happy child lived on in her anyway, yet as in the dream, a paternal authority figure was at work inside her that prohibited her from expressing this side of herself in a free and untroubled way. She was a very serious person and tended to block joyful and mischievous feelings. As in the dream, inwardly she could not assert herself enough to let the childlike side of her express itself. But that was to change. Increasingly, happy and boisterous children appeared in her dreams. Here is an example.

> From the window of a house I watch as a girl about five years old with curly brown hair and a boy of the same age slide on their stomachs in the garden. They are enjoying this a great deal. I am enjoying watching them too. Then I am standing in front of a store. The little girl comes out beaming with delight because she has bought something on her own, all by herself. I am not much larger than the child myself.

These children are happy, too, and slide around in the mud. Their pleasure is similar to that of the little girl in the previous dream, but this time no one intervenes. On the contrary, the action continues and culminates in the girl's independent purchase. The dreamer shares her happiness. That she herself is not much larger than the child could indicate that the experi-

ence of being a child in this way was brought close to home for
her very literally.

In the dream the joyous sliding in the mud is connected
with the little girl's independent step of getting something for
herself in the store. Her fun can be viewed as the beginning
of world mastery. Children practice their potentialities in free
play and thus can experience and get to know their own limits
and those of others. In this way the foundation for the courage
to do something freely and independently is laid. Children
who are restricted too much, who are overprotected and allowed no freedom of play, tend to become overly obedient and
have no confidence in their ability to take independent steps.
They imitate adult behavior very early and well, but avoid unknown situations and have little courage in the face of the new
and unknown.

Gradually, among Erna's dreams, those became more numerous in which children could give free rein to their play impulses
and sense of enjoyment and were no longer threatened by brutally punitive adults. In them, Erna uncovered the carefree style
of experience that had not been granted her as a child. In this
process it was interesting to see that the adult masculine figures
changed and—as in the following dream—participated in the
children's fun:

> An infant and a large, ungainly man make a great leap toward
> me in the bathtub. The infant dives under the suds, but I
> catch him in the crook of my arm and wash the suds off his
> face. He laughs with his whole face as though he has suc-
> ceeded at something.

Often we are able to reclaim experiences in dreams of a sort
we have never had or experienced too little in real life. By
making contact—first in the dreams—with certain childlike aspects of herself, Erna "rehearsed" behaviors that she learned to
live out increasingly in her everyday life. In this way her seri-
ousness, which was fine in itself, was tempered by spontaneity
and fun, making her whole demeanor appear brighter and more
exuberant.

The Creative Core

Alex, whom I discussed in the preceding chapter, once had the following dream:

> I am writing about the conception of a child, about pregnancy and birth. But it is precisely the act of writing that brings about these processes. Now that I am finished, I feel like a new man.

This brief dream contains several remarkable aspects. The child and the creative act are represented as closely connected with each other here. The creative activity of writing is understood as a process of procreation and birth and ultimately, after the successful "birth" of his product, causes the author to feel like a new man. Creative activity is like having a child; in fact, people often speak of someone's creation as his "child."

The creative act is ultimately understood as a process of rebirth, as an emotional-spiritual renewal. Alex, whom we met as a serious, conscientious person, integrated more and more childlike aspects of himself in the course of his analysis—his spontaneity, his sense of happiness, his healthy, natural wit— and devoted himself increasingly to playful activities. These changes also enabled Alex to become more creative. The newly won inner freedom made it possible for him to create intellectual connections in a relaxed fashion, to recognize intellectual relationships and express them in writing. The strict, academic had given way to a freer, creative person. A *Homo creativus* appeared beside the *Homo sapiens*. This transition was able to take place through a process of play.

In play we are engaged but without a goal. Through this engagement, free from constraint and serious objectives, we often find solutions that prove to be new and genuinely creative. In play we are in the moment and completely devoted to the matter at hand, we are absorbed in play. The Dutch cultural philosopher Johan Huizinga coined an appropriate new expression for the person at play: *Homo ludens* (Lat. *ludere*, to play). This concept really only takes on full meaning, however, through its proximity to concepts such as *Homo faber* (the practical, technically endowed person) and *Homo sapiens* (the person endowed with reason, also the academic characterization of modern man). These latter two associate existence with technology and reason, both highly esteemed values today. *Homo ludens* designates a third, independent category and extends our image of humanity into the creative realm. According to Huizinga's exposition (which is quite worth reading), all culture and the capacity for every cultural achievement are based in the final analysis on play and thus on a frame of mind in which the person feels engaged but free and is "outside of the process of indirect satisfaction of needs and desires."[14] In the realm of play, outside of the serious and dutiful fulfillment of life's needs, the first beginnings of creative activity and culture arise.

Many people, stressed by work, have lost the capacity for profound absorption in play and are hardly able anymore to abandon themselves playfully in inner freedom to anything with heart and soul. The child still has this ability to a large extent. By means of his fantasies, he can set himself above reality, make it a part of his ideas, and playfully and creatively lose himself in this world of imagination. Thus he can sit in the first chair of a long row of chairs and play engineer and railroad, without feeling any limits on his imaginative fancies. The difference between the play world and the everyday world becomes fully clear when a playing child is interrupted. Once a mother said to her young daughter who was playing teacher with her doll that she should wash the dishes. "Mommy," the little girl said, "you can't order me to do that, because my students will think I'm not a real teacher!" The child at play is completely fulfilled inwardly and is even capable of disregarding an oppressive reality. In this connection, I think of Bernhard, who made up games that he played with an imaginary partner. These games consoled him in his loneliness and allowed him even to forget it at times.

As adults we have to a large extent lost the capacity for such absorption. However, we can experience it anew in creative activity. Therefore, it is not by chance that dreams also use the symbol of the child in the context of playful, creative activities.

In the dream of Dora, a forty-two-year-old woman, such a child appears and imparts the feeling of blessed surrender to the observing adult:

> I enter a room with my husband. It is my brother's room in our parents' former home. There is a high, old-fashioned bed. In the bed, buried in many covers and pillows, a child is playing contentedly. Completely absorbed, she sings songs and melodies to herself. The scene is extremely touching, and we remain standing in the doorway, absorbed in looking at the child. Then I go over to the child. We knew this was our child, and yet at the same time, it wasn't her. The child is about three years old. She has an injured eye, the tip of her nose is injured, and she has blue bruise marks. The child's happiness is overwhelming, contagious, and extremely profound.

This dream appeared when Dora was experiencing herself as inwardly disoriented and had lost her center. Creatively gifted, she expressed her talent in painting. At the time she was in a barren period; the creative energy would not flow, and she experienced herself as blocked. The room in the dream was the brother's childhood room in their parents' house. Her brother, likewise a gifted personality, in addition to being employed as an engineer, remained active as a writer. The dream led Dora into her childhood and thus into the realm of her gifted brother. It also evoked the sense of a creative source in her childhood. The child, her own yet not her own, plays contentedly by herself and is so absorbed in her play world that she does not notice the approach of the adults nor even her own injuries. The injured child represented Dora's creative side, which was in fact experienced in her waking life as wounded and did not function anymore. In the dream this side appears again, now fully active, and captivates Dora and her husband. The dream made her feel happy and brought about a mood change. In the depths of her soul the connection to her creative possibilities had been recovered. In the period that followed, her creative energy began to flow once more.

Erich, a technician who decided late in life to get his high school diploma and study architecture, also dreamed about children in connection with his creative orientation:

> I am in the high school library and have just given birth to
> twins. The librarian is there too, and she is pleased about the
> children, who are already awake.

In school, Erich had to study art history and do readings on
related topics. At the time of the dream, he was busy writing a
seminar paper on a theme connected to urban development.
Because he did not have confidence in doing academic work, he
felt a certain anxiety about the new task. The dream consoled
him, however, and immediately made him a gift of children in
the library, the place where he would later be spending a lot of
time. The twins represented his work and symbolized his creative potential.

Apart from that, the dream is an excellent example of the fact
that men can have birth dreams and in them can experience
labor pains and the corresponding joys otherwise reserved for
women. All the same, I must add that men giving birth in
dreams is relatively rare, whereas among women, in accordance
with their nature, such dreams frequently occur.

Our creative potential is often threatened. These threats generally arise from inside our own psyches. Fears, doubts, and
thoughts of authorities who know and can do things better sometimes seriously inhibit our undertakings. A critique from outside
can also cause our self-esteem to falter dangerously and perhaps
fall to very low levels. Without a certain degree of self-esteem, no
creative achievements are possible. We lack the necessary im-
petus and entangle ourselves in a web of pessimistic fantasies.

This is what happened to Barbara when she had to take her
final examinations to become a teacher after a seemingly endless
period of preparation. As tends to happen, she felt drained and
unable to do another thing. Her unconscious assessed this situation differently, however, and balanced out her low self-
esteem through the symbol of the child. She had the following
dream.

> In my parents' bedroom in my mother's bed lies a sweet
> newborn baby. On entering the room, I am prepared for the
> little one to start crying, but this does not happen. On the
> contrary, he laughs at me and starts to talk. I have to go to an

exam, and it turns out that he knows almost as much as I do
about the subject. He has also become somewhat bigger, so
that he can walk, and we walk together to the exam. But he
is still a small child of about five. I am convinced that the boy
can accomplish a great deal professionally later, since he
already knows so much as such a small child.

Among other things, the child in the dream stands for the
knowledge accumulated through long months. He laughs in the
dream, and Barbara decides to go to the exam with him. It was
important for her, in connection with the dream, to return to a
sense of enjoying the material, to remember the enthusiasm with
which she had originally begun her studies. The child in the
dream—her inner child—is not afraid; he is happy and, thanks
to his youthful energy, will be able to react creatively during the
exam and answer questions without fear. Connection to such a
child is something we all need in situations that test us.

A threat to our creative side can also show itself in dreams.
Hans-Martin, who had just worked out a graphics presentation
for a commercial, suddenly saw his work as completely unusable
and did not dare show it to his employer. He began to rework
everything late at night, but was not able to come up with
anything better and sank into a sea of anxieties and doubts. One
night he dreamed:

A child is lying in a casket in a grave. They intend to bury
him. The priest, dressed all in black, is already there and
begins to say the burial liturgy. I rush to the still-open casket
and lift the child out because I am convinced that he is still
alive.

This dream made Hans-Martin conscious of the fact that he was
on the verge of burying the product of his creative work. It
changed his mind, and he took the risk of presenting the work
to his boss, who accepted it with pleasure.

Women in particular are inclined to undermine their own
creative potential. Since it has not been so long since women
have been able to receive higher levels of education and be
trained professionally, they are particularly susceptible to crit-
icism and sometimes feel less secure than men, whose partici-

pation in creative activities has never been questioned. The patriarchal orientation of our society causes women often to believe that they have to solve problems in a detached way, as men do. But women often approach projects differently—more emotionally, irrationally, and indirectly. Yet just in these specific feminine attitudes, they let themselves be disturbed by masculine ideas such as having to be goal-oriented and objective. Thus they often let their plans fall by the wayside.

Monica, whom I discussed in the section "A Childhood Marked by Illness" (chapter 1), allowed herself to be bothered in her work again and again by the thought that a man, or a particular male colleague, could handle the young patients better than she and would work with them differently. To be sure, they probably would work with them differently. But it was important for Monica to be conscious of her own feminine way of seeing herself and to allow intuition, imagination, and feeling in her work. Only in this way could she generate good ideas and feel animated about her work. As she repeatedly let herself be buried by masculine objectives, she dreamed the following instructive dream:

> I enter into a Gothic city of stone that has been in existence for ages. Wide underground rooms, terribly dark, everything petrified. I know one has to go through it, step by step, which I do with great tenacity and persistence. Then I come to a large black gaping gateway. I believe I can get through it. But then a window closes around my throat with an iron grip. It is a nightmare—how am I supposed to free myself? Then it occurs to me that I can depend on my inner voice, and in this moment everything is resolved, everything is saved. People and life stream toward me, a woman thanks me for deliverance. Then a small blond child is handed to me. I hug her close to me. A man is a part of this, and I feel great closeness to him and to the child.

Monica interpreted the Gothic city of stone as the masculine world. Actually the Gothic style, with its slender architecture rising into the air, possesses a typical masculine orientation. The Gothic style strives toward the light, toward heaven, in an attempt to escape the earth's gravity, which was still very much a part of the Romanesque style. Monica fights her way tenaciously through this petrified stone city but does not feel that she is in her element. In reality Monica had diligently acquired masculine tools in her education, was capable of thinking logically and recognizing objective facts. But through this her feelings fell into the background, and she became alienated from herself. In the dream a window closes around her throat, and she feels close to suffocating. However, at the moment when she remembers her inner voice, everything is resolved and life streams toward her. Her regained sense of being alive culminates in the symbol of the child. The child stands for *joie de vivre* and creative orientation in general. She accepts it lovingly and thus comes into contact with a man who is fond of her and to whom she would like to belong. It is extremely important that women develop an animus, a masculine side in themselves, that affirms and values the specifically feminine capacities. Only then can they get fully involved in their creative potential and give it the space it needs to develop.

The creative element is not symbolized only by children. Frequently it is symbolized by a dwarf or gnome. Gnomes are earth spirits that live in and under the earth. They are mostly old, wrinkled, and bearded. They typically wear a red pointed cap. Underground they guard treasures and unearth metals and precious stones. Often they are excellent smiths and know a lot about cooking and baking. Gnomes usually have a positive meaning, and the ugly gnome seldom crops up. Gnomes as a rule intend good things for people, reward their good deeds with generous gifts, and often turn out to be genuine helpers.[15]

Their preoccupation with underground work and their ability to produce beautiful works in metal make gnomes part of the realm of the Great Mother and indicate the highest degree of creativity. The little beings appear in Greek mythology as dactyls (Greek *daktylos* = finger) and Cabiri and are affiliated with the mother goddesses Cybele, Rhea, and Adresleia.[16]

If we are creative, then we have access to the Great Mother who brings forth all life. The Great Mother works in the realm of the unconscious, from which the creative germ arises in dreams and fantasies and waits to be taken over by daytime consciousness.

The creative person has a special connection to the feminine and the unconscious, to the processes of growth, development, birth, and new life. To be genuinely creative we must first involve ourselves in these processes, opening up to creative inspiration without having a specific goal in mind. Receiving inspiration requires a feminine attitude of expectant receptivity.

How much the gnome, as a variation of the child motif, is bound up with creative inspiration is shown quite beautifully in the following events recounted to me by a woman named Ruth. She had been alone once in the month of November in her vacation home in Switzerland, far from civilization, and had been able to abandon herself completely to her thoughts and to the world of nature. No traffic and no restaurant noise intruded upon her peaceful solitude. No telephone could disturb the calm either, because the house did not have a private connection. The closest telephone, in the village, was out of order and being repaired at the time. One night, she recalled, she began to dream and then had the feeling that someone wanted to rouse her from sleep. Then she saw a little gnome dressed in green who was cheerfully springing to and fro on her bed over her hips, giving her back little nudges as though he wanted to say something to her. Should she get up and open the door for him? She dismissed the thought because it was so cold in the room and the gnome would probably find his own way out. Then she went back to sleep.

The next morning she had the strong feeling that something had happened. She got dressed and packed, went to the railroad station, and took a train home. She had hardly arrived when the telephone rang and she was told that her godfather, of whom she had been very fond, had died. Because her godfather lived in Hamburg instead of in Switzerland, the funeral was taking place there. Thanks to the gnome's message she had enough time to reach the funeral on time. The gnome of her inner vision was a true helper. He knew more than her conscious mind and communicated knowledge to her that could not have been available to her waking consciousness.

In the following dream of Erika's, the gnome appears in closer relation to the child, showing that the dwarf, the child, and the creative impulse are connected by an inner relationship.

> I was on the way home in my car. Then I was standing in the street, and out of the asphalt grew a dwarfish little squirt dressed in a fire-red little robe. He resembled Mark, my child.

Like a real gnome or one of the Cabiri, the childlike being surfaces out of the depths of the earth. In doing this he manages to break through the solid asphalt without injury. The little squirt had a great deal to do with Erika's creative potential, which she had endeavored to reactivate after her child had grown older. The unconscious accommodated her and greeted her plans with the figure of the little man dressed in vermilion, her favorite color. Red is also a signal color. The gnome was giving Erika the signal to get on with the undertakings she had planned and in breaking through the asphalt gave her the sign of an auspicious beginning.

Finding the child in ourselves means making contact with the child we once were, achieving closeness to our own innate nature, and ultimately becoming aware of our creative potentialities, the development of which always plays an essential role in shaping our future.

Notes

INTRODUCTION

1. D. von Gersdorf, *Kinderbildnisse aus vier Jahrtausenden* (Berlin: Edition Hentrich, Frölich & Kaufman, n.d.), p. 21.
2. Quoted in D. Lenzen, *Mythologie der Kindheit* (Reinbek b. Hamburg: Rowohlt Verlag, 1985), p. 200f.
3. See H. Rühfel, *Das Kind in der griechischen Kunst* (Mainz: Verlag Philipp von Zabern, 1984).
4. Ibid., p. 174.
5. E. Trube-Becker, *Gewalt gegen das Kind: Vernachlässigung Misshandlung, sexueller Missbrauch und Tötung von Kindern* (Heidelberg: Kriminalistik Verlag, 1982), p. 7.
6. Cf. Kathrin Asper, *Verlassenheit und Selbstentfremdung* (Olten & Freiburg i. Br.: Walter Verlag, 1987).
7. Johann Wolfgang von Goethe, *Dichtung und Wahrheit,* in *Werke in zwei Bände,* vol. 1 (Salzburg: Das Berglandbuch, 1953), p. 55.
8. Asper, *Verlassenheit und Selbstentfremdung.*
9. Goethe, p. 96.

CHAPTER 1. THE CHILD AND CHILDHOOD IN DREAMS

1. Sigmund Freud, *Psychopsathologie des Alltagslebens (The Psychopathology of Everyday Life),* vol. 4, *Gesammelten Werke* (Frankfurt am Main: Fischer Verlag, 1941), p. 51.
2. Cf. Mario Jacoby, *Psychotherapeuten sind auch Menschen: Übertragung und menschliche Beziehung in der Jungschen Praxis* (Olten and Freiburg i. Br.: Walter Verlag, 1987).
3. Cf. E. Drewermann, "Das Mädchen ohne Hände," *Grimms Märchen tiefenpsychologisch gedeutet* (Olten & Freiburg i. Br.: Walter Verlag, 1987).
4. H. Bachtold-Staubli (ed.), *Handwörterbuch des deutschen Aberglaubens* (Berlin & Leipzig: Walter de Gruyter, 1927ff.). vol. 6, cols. 1361ff.
5. Cf. Asper, *Verlassenheit und Selbstentfremdung.*
6. John Bowlby, *Verlust, Trauer und Depression* (Frankfurt a.M.: Fischer Verlag, 1983). *Loss* (New York: Basic Books, 1982).
7. Cf. Bowlby, *Separation* and *Loss.*
8. Cf. Asper, *Verlassenheit und Selbstentfremdung.*
9. See D. W. Winicott, *Vom Spiel zur Kreativität* (Stuttgart: Klett-Cotta, 1979), pp. 128ff.
10. See Jolande Jacobi, *Die Psychologie von C. G. Jung (The Psychology of C. G. Jung)* (Olten & Freiburg i. Br.: Walter Verlag, 1987), pp. 5–77.

Chapter 2. The Child as a Symbol of Life

1. Cf. P. Kielholz, *Diagnose und Therapie der Depression für den Praktiker* (Munich: J. F. Lehmanns Verlag, 1971), and D. Widlöcher, *Die Depression* (Munich: Piper Verlag, 1986).
2. See R. Klibansky, E. Panofsky, and F. Saxl, *Saturn and Melancholy* (London: Nelson, 1964), p. 343 f.
3. Romano Guardini, *Vom Sinn der Schwermut* (Mainz: Matthias Grünewalt Verlag, 1983), p. 31.
4. Quoted in ibid., p. 14.
5. E. Norden, *Die Geburt des Kindes* (Leipzig & Berlin: Teubner Verlag, 1924), pp. 9–10.

Chapter 3. The Divine and Holy Child

1. M. Kiessig (ed.), *Dichter erzählen ihre Träume* (Stuttgart: Verlag Urachhaus, 1976), p. 155.
2. Cf. Helmut Hark, *Vom Kirchentraum zur Traum-Kirche* (Olten & Freiburg i. Br.: Walter Verlag, 1987.
3. Cf. J. Canacakis, *Ich sehe Deine Tränen: Klagen, trauern, leben können* (Stuttgart: Kreuz Verlag, 1987).
4. A courageous woman, Ursula Goldmann-Posch, published a frank account of her own depression in which thoughts of abuse similar in content to those of Sabine appeared. In this honest portrayal she makes the inner experience and external difficulties of depression accessible to others. U. Goldmann-Posch, *Tagebuch einer Depression* (Munich: Kindler Verlag, 1985).
5. Cf. Kathrin Asper, "Der therapeutischen Storung," *Analyt. Psychol.* 17 (1986):1–25; Jolande Jacobi, *Die Psychologie von C. G. Jung*, pp. 168ff.
6. Guardini, p. 7.
7. C. G. Jung, "Zur Psychologie des Kindarchetypus" (1940/1951), *GW* 9/1 (Olten & Freiburg i. Br.: Walter Verlag, 1976), pp. 173–174.
8. Mircea Eliade et al., *Die Schöpferungsmythen* (Darmstadt: Wissenschaftliche Buchgesellschaft, 1980), p. 6.
9. Ibid., p. 132.
10. Ibid., p. 147.
11. Cf. Karl Kerényi, "Das göttliche Kind," in C. G. Jung and Karl Kerényi, *Das göttliche Kind* (Leipzig: Pantheon Akademische Verlagsanstalt, 1940).
12. Eliade, p. 76.
13. Ibid., pp. 79–80.
14. Ibid., p. 137.
15. P. Schwarzenau, *Das göttliche Kind* (Stuttgart: Kreuz Verlag, 1984), pp. 47–48.
16. Translated from A. Weiher (ed.), *Homerische Hymnen* (Munich: Heimeran Verlag, 1970), p. 63.
17. Cf. R. Amman, *Traumbild Haud* (Olten & Freiburg i. Br.: Walter Verlag, 1987).

18. D. Gaudenz, *Erinnerungen eines Landarztes* (Chur: Calven Verlag, 1974), pp. 248–249.
19. C. Edvardson, *Gebranntes Kind sucht das Feuer* (Vienna: Carl Hanser Verlag, 1986), pp. 92–93.

CHAPTER 4.   THE CHILD OF GOD

1. Cf. K.-H. Mallet, *Untertan Kind: Nachforschungen über Erziehung* (Ismaning b. Munich: Verlag Max Hueber, 1987).
2. Quoted in ibid., p. 44.
3. Jung, p. 176.
4. Cf. RGG, *Die Religion in Geschichte und Gegenwart*, ed. K. Galling, (Tübingen: Mohr Verlag, 1958), vol. 2, cols. 1799ff.
5. Paul Tillich, *Das neue Sein* (Stuttgart: Evangelisches Verlagswerk, 1959), p. 76. *The New Being* (New York: Scribner, 1955).
6. Jung, p. 184.

CHAPTER 5.   THE SMILING CHILD

1. E. Norden, *Die Geburt des Kindes* (Leipzig & Berlin: Teubner Verlag, 1924), p. 10.
2. D. Lenzen, *Mythologie der Kindheit* (Reinbek b. Hamburg: Rowohlt Verlag, 1985), 206.
3. Bachtold-Staubli (ed.), *Handwörterbuch des deutschen Aberglaubens*, vol. 5, col. 877.
4. E. Hennecke, *Neutestamentliche Apokryphen*, ed. W. Schneemelcher, vol. 1 (Tübingen: Mohr [Siebeck] Verlag, 1959), p. 293f.
5. *Provenzalische Märchen*, ed. & trans. F. Karlinger and G. Greciano (Düsseldorf & Cologne: Diederichs Verlag, 1974), no. 37, p. 181f.
6. Wilhelm Busch, *Wilhelm Busch: Die schönsten Bildesgeschichten für die Jugend* (Munich: Sudwest Verlag, n.d.), p. 9.
7. Ibid., p. 9.
8. Cf. Mallet, p. 298; D. Richter, *Das fremde Kind: Zur Entstehung der Kindheitsbilder des bürgerlichen Zeitalters* (Frankfurt a.M.: Fischer Verlag, 1987), p. 107.
9. *Staubs Kinderbüchlein* (St. Gallen: Fehrsche Verlagsanstalt, n.d.), p. 4.
10. Ibid., p. 12.
11. Ibid., p. 210.
12. F. K. Waechter, *Der Anti-Struwwelpeter* (Zurich: Diogenes Verlag, 1970), p. 19.
13. Ibid., p. 20.
14. J. Huizinga, *Homo ludens: Vom Ursprung der Kultur im Spiel* (Munich: Rowohlt Verlag, 1961), p. 16. *Homo Ludens: A Study of the Play Element in Culture* (Boston: Beacon Press, 1955).
15. Bachtold-Staubli, vol. 9, cols. 1008ff.
16. Pauly the Younger, *Lexikon der Antike*, 5 vols. (Munich: Deutscher Taschenbuch Verlag, 1979), vol. 1, cols. 363ff.; vol. 3, cols. 34ff.

Glossary

ANIMA, ANIMUS   The anima represents the feminine image in the man, the animus the masculine image in the woman. The conscious realization of these archetypal components of the psyche is necessitated by the process of *individuation*.

ARCHETYPE, ARCHETYPAL   (Greek = prototype, primordial image) Forms of perceptual interpretation and action that appear within the psyche as symbols and manifest in the instincts. Transcending the individual personality, archetypal images appear in religions, mythologies, literature, and art.

COLLECTIVE UNCONSCIOUS   The collective unconscious represents the primordial experiences and images of humanity that are independent of personal experiences. The contents of the collective unconscious are the *archetypes*.

COMPLEX   (Latin *complectere*, to interweave) A feeling-toned group of ideas in the unconscious. Bringing complexes to consciousness has a liberating and healing effect. As a rule complexes arise in childhood and become part of the *personal unconscious*. Their core is, however, *archetypal* in nature. If the archetypal element breaks through into consciousness, the ego is overwhelmed, bringing about a state of possession.

COUNTERTRANSFERENCE   In the narrow sense, the reactions of the analyst to the analysand. This can be connected with the analysand but can also be completely illusory, related only to the personality of the analyst.

FATHER ARCHETYPE   This archetype conditions all paternal qualities and expressions. The child encounters it first in the personal father and later in authority figures and in patriarchally determined institutions.

GREAT FATHER   *See* Father archetype.

GREAT MOTHER   *See* Mother archetype.

INDIVIDUATION   A process of self-development that leads the individual to the most complete possible realization of his or her inborn potential.

MOTHER ARCHETYPE   This archetype encompasses all maternal and feminine qualities and expressions. The child encounters it first in the personal mother and later in feminine caregiving figures and in nature as the suprapersonal mother.

NEUROSIS   In general terms, an unsuccessfully resolved conflict whose roots go back to childhood. Compulsive, anxiety, and hysterical neuroses are distinguished. According to Jung the conflict is not so much confined to childhood as represented in the current situation. From the Jungian point of view, neurosis always provides an opportunity for wholesome change.

PERSONA   One adapts to society by means of the persona. Identification with the persona is dangerous because it becomes a mask that obstructs realization of the wholeness of the personality.

PERSONAL UNCONSCIOUS   The forgotten and subliminally experienced contents of one's own individual past.

PROJECTION   An unconscious process by which one's own inner qualities and aspects of one's personality are exteriorized and localized in another person or thing.

SELF   A central *archetype* that includes the entire psyche, that is, the psychobiological totality that directs the development of life cycles and is at the same time the goal of *individuation*. The Self is the image of God in the soul and the psychic "organ" for the perception of the divine and the eternal.

SHADOW   It incorporates the unconscious aspects of personality that are inferior, obscure, and undeveloped. They are for the most part repressed and therefore manifest negatively. The shadow includes the *personal unconscious*, but extends beyond that into the *collective unconscious*.

SYMBOL   The best possible representation and formulation of something still unknown. Whether something is a symbol or not depends on the attitude of the observer. The symbol is bound up with intuition and emotional apprehension and points to a meaning that cannot yet be more closely delineated.

TRANSFERENCE   In a narrow sense, a particular form of *projection*. In transference, the experiences that one had with one's parents and other close ones are unconsciously reexperienced in relation to the analyst and are reproduced anew. These repetitions of the past are not really directed toward the analyst but rather toward the people in these earlier relationships. Thanks to the feelings that arise in transference, the analysand's childhood can be understood and worked through. Transference in the broader sense is based on the *archetypes*. Thus, behind one's parents and one's experiences of and about them stand the *father archetype* and the *mother archetype*.

UNCONSCIOUS   *See* collective unconscious; personal unconscious.

Bibliography

Amman, R. *Traumbild Haus.* Olten & Freiburg i. Br.: Walter-Verlag, 1987.

Ariès, Philippe. *Geschichte der Kindheit.* Munich: Deutscher Taschenbuchverlag, 1982.

Asper, Kathrin. "Der therapeutische Umgang mit Schattenaspekten der narzisstischen Storung." *Analyt. Psychol.* 17 (1986): 1–25.

————. *Verlassenheit und Selbstentfremdung.* Olten & Freibug i. Br.: Walter Verlag, 1987.

Badinter, E. *Die Mutterliebe: Geschichte eines Gefühls vom 17. Jahrhundert bis heute.* Munich: Pipe Verlag, 1981.

Bachtold-Staubli, H. (ed.). *Handwörterbuch des deutschen Aberglaubens.* Berlin & Leipzig: Walter de Gruyter, 1927 ff.

Bowlby, John. *Loss.* New York: Basic Books, 1982.

————. *Separation: Anxiety and Anger* (New York: Basic Books, 1973).

Busch, Wilhelm. *Wilhelm Busch: Die schönsten Bildgeschichten fur die Jugend.* Munich: Sudwest Verlag, n. d.

Canacakis, J. *Ich sehe Deine Tränen: Klagen, trauern, leben können.* Stuttgart: Kreuz Verlag, 1987.

de Mause, L. (ed.). *Hört ihr die Kinder weinen.* Frankfurt a.M: Suhrkamp Verlag, 1982.

Drewermann, E. *Das Mädchen ohne Hände: Grimms Märchen tiefenpsychologisch gedeutet.* Olten & Freiburg i. Br.: Walter Verlag, 1987.

————. *Marienkind: Grimms Märchen tiefenpsychologisch gedeutet.* Olten & Freiburg i. Br.: Walter Verlag, 1985.

Edvardson, C. *Gebranntes Kind sucht das Feuer.* Vienna: Carl Hanser Verlag, 1986.

Eliade, Mircea, et al. *Die Schöpfungsmythen.* Darmstadt: Wissenschaftliche Buchgesellschaft, 1980.

Freud, Sigmund. *Psychopathologie des Alltagslebens,* vol. 4 of *Gesammelten Werke.* Frankfurt a.M.: Fischer Verlag, 1941. *Psychopathology of Everyday Life,* ed. James Strachey. New York: Norton, 1971.

Gaudenz, D.: *Erinnerungen eines Landarztes.* Chur: Calven Verlag, 1974.

Gersdorf, D. von. *Kinderbildnisse aus vier Jahrtausenden.* Berlin: Edition Hentrich, Frölich und Kaufmann, n.d.

Goethe, Johann Wolfgang von. *Dichtung und Wahrheit.* In *Werke in zwei Bänden,* vol. 1. Salzburg: Das Berglandbuch, 1953.

Goldmann-Posch, U. *Tagebuch einer Depression.* Munich: Kindler Verlag, 1985.

Guardini, R. *Vom Sinn der Schwermut.* Mainz: Matthias Grünewalt Verlag, 1983.

Grimm Brothers. *Kinder- und Hausmärchen* (1857), 3 vols. Stuttgart: Reclam Verlag, 1980.

Hark, Helmut. *Vom Kirchentraum zur Traum-Kirche.* Olten & Freiburg i. Br.: Walter Verlag, 1987.

Hennecke, E. *Neutestamentliche Apokryphen,* ed. W. Schneemelcher, vol. 1 Tübingen: Mohr (Siebeck) Verlag, 1959.

Hoffman, H. *Das Struwwelpeter-Album.* Frankfurt a.M.: Rütten und Loening Verlag, n.d.

Huizinga, Johan. *Homo Ludens: A Study of the Play Element in Culture,* Boston: Beacon Press, 1955.

Jacobi, Jolande. *The Psychology of C. G. Jung,* tr. Ralph Manheim. New Haven: Yale University Press, 1973.

Jacoby, Mario. *Psychotherapeuten sind auch Menschen: Übertragung und menschliche Beziehung in der Jungschen Praxis.* Olten & Freiburg i. Br.: Walter Verlag, 1987.

Jung, C. G. *Zur Psychologie des Kindarchetypus* (1940/1951), in *GW* 9/1. Olten & Freiburg i. Br.: Walter Verlag, 1976.

Kaschnitz, M.-L. *Die Gedichte. Gesammelte Werke,* vol. 5. Frankfurt a.M.: Insel Verlag, 1985.

Kerényi, Karl. *Das göttliche Kind,* in C. G. Jung and Karl Kerényi, *Das göttliche Kind.* Leipzig: Pantheon Akademische Verlagsanstalt, 1940.

Kielholz, P. *Diagnose und Therapie der Depressionen für den Praktiker.* Munich: J. F. Lehmanns Verlag, 1971.

Kiessig, M. (ed.). *Dichter erzählen ihre Träume.* Stuttgart: Verlag Urachhaus, 1976.

Klibansky, R.; Panofsky, E.; and Saxl, F. *Saturn and Melancholy.* London: Nelson, 1964.

Lenzen, D. *Mythologie der Kindheit.* Reinbek bei Hamburg: Rowohlt Verlag, 1985.

Mallet, K.-H *Untertan Kind: Nachforschungen über Erziehung.* Ismaning b. Munich: Verlag Max Hueber, 1987.

Norden, E. *Die Geburt des Kindes.* Leipzig & Berlin: Teubner Verlag, 1924.

Neumann, Erich. *The Great Mother: An Analysis of the Archetype,* tr. Ralph Manheim. New Haven: Princeton University Press, 1964.

Pauly (the Younger). *Lexikon der Antike.* 5 vols. Munich: Deutscher Taschenbuch Verlag, 1979.

Provenzalische Märchen, ed. & trans. F. Karlinger and G. Gréciano. Düsseldorf & Köln: Diederichs Verlag, 1974.

RGG. *Die Religion in Geschichte und Gegenwart,* ed. K. Galling. Vol. 2. Tübingen: Mohr Verlag, 1958.

Richter, D. *Das fremde Kind: Zur Entstehung der Kindheitsbilder des bürgerlichen Zeitalters.* Frankfurt a.M.: Fischer Verlag, 1987.

Rühfel, H. *Das Kind in der griechischen Kunst.* Mainz: Verlag Philipp von Zabern, 1984.

Rutschky, K. *Schwarze Pädagogik: Quellen zur Naturgeschichte der bürgerlichen Erziehung.* Frankfurt a.M.: Ullstein Verlag, 1987.

Schwarzenau, P. *Das göttliche Kind.* Stuttgart: Kreuz Verlag, 1984.

Staubs Kinderbüchlein. St. Gallen: Fehrsche Verlagsanstalt, n.d.

Tillich, Paul. *The Courage to Be.* New Haven: Yale University Press, 1952.

————. *The New Being*. New York: Scribner, 1955.

Trube-Becker, E. *Gewalt gegen das Kind: Vernachlässigung, Misshandlung, sexueller Missbrauch und Tötung von Kindern*. Heidelberg: Kriminalistik Verlag, 1982.

Waechter, F. K. *Der Anti-Struwwelpeter*. Zurich: Diogenes Verlag, 1982.

Weiher, A. (ed.). *Homerische Hymnen*. Munich: Heimeran Verlag, 1970.

Widlöcher, D. *Die Depression*. Munich: Piper Verlag, 1986.

Winnicott, D. W. *Vom Spiel zur Kreativität*. Stuttgart: Klett-Cotta, 1979.

OTHER C. G. JUNG FOUNDATION BOOKS FROM SHAMBHALA PUBLICATIONS

Absent Fathers, Lost Sons: The Search for Masculine Identity,
by Guy Corneau

*The Child, by Erich Neumann.
Foreword by Louis H. Stewart.

Cross-Currents of Jungian Thought: An Annotated Biography,
by Donald R. Dyer.

*Depth Psychology and a New Ethic, by Erich Neumann.
Forewords by C. G. Jung, Gerhard Adler,
and James Yandell.

*Dreams, by Marie-Louise von Franz.

**From Freud to Jung: A Comparative Study of the Psychology
of the Unconscious,* by Liliane Frey-Rohn.
Foreword by Robert Hinshaw.

A Guided Tour of the Collected Works *of C. G. Jung,* by
Robert H. Hopcke. Foreword by Aryeh Maidenbaum.

Individuation in Fairy Tales, Revised Edition,
by Marie-Louise von Franz.

*In Her Image: The Unhealed Daughter's Search for Her
Mother,* by Kathie Carlson.

Knowing Woman: A Feminine Psychology,
by Irene Claremont de Castillejo.

Lingering Shadows: Jungians, Freudians, and Anti-Semitism,
edited by Aryeh Maidenbaum and Stephen A. Martin.

The Old Wise Woman: A Study of Active Imagination,
by Rix Weaver. Introduction by C. A. Meier.

*Power and Politics: The Psychology of Soviet-American Part-
nership,* by Jerome S. Bernstein. Forewords by Senator
Clairborne Pell and Edward C. Whitmont, M.D.

The Way of All Women, by M. Esther Harding.
Introduction by C. G. Jung.

The Wisdom of the Dream: The World of C. G. Jung,
by Stephen Segaller and Merrill Berger.

Woman's Mysteries: Ancient and Modern,
by M. Esther Harding. Introduction by C. G. Jung.

*Published in association with Daimon Verlag, Einsiedeln,
Switzerland.